PYROMETRY

CHAPTER I
INTRODUCTION

The term "pyrometer"—formerly applied to instruments designed to measure the expansion of solids—is now used to describe any device for determining temperatures beyond the upper limit of a mercury thermometer. This limit, in the common form, is the boiling point of mercury: 357° C. or 672° F. By leaving the bore of the tube full of nitrogen or carbon dioxide prior to sealing, the pressure exerted by the enclosed gas when the mercury expands prevents boiling; and with a strong bulb of hard glass the readings may be extended to 550° C. or 1020° F. Above this temperature the hardest glass is distorted by the high internal pressure, but, by substituting silica for glass, readings as high as 700° C. or 1290° F. may be secured. Whilst such thermometers are useful in laboratory processes they are too fragile for workshop use; and if made of the length necessary in many cases in which the temperature of furnaces is sought, the cost would be as great as that of more durable and convenient appliances. No other instrument, however, is so simple to read as the thermometer; and for this reason it is used whenever the conditions are favourable. The latest proposal in this direction is due to Northrup, who has constructed a thermometer containing tin enclosed in a graphite envelope, which is capable of reading up to 1500° C. or higher. This instrument is described on page 216.

The origin and development of the science of pyrometry furnish a notable example of the value of the application of scientific principles to industry. Sir Isaac Newton was the first to attempt to measure the temperature of a fire by observing the time taken to cool by a bar of iron withdrawn from the fire; but, although Newton's results were published in 1701, it was not until 1782 that a practical instrument for measuring high temperatures was designed. In that year Josiah Wedgwood, the famous potter, introduced an instrument based on the progressive contraction undergone by clay when baked at increasing temperatures, which he used in controlling his furnaces, finding it much more reliable than the eye of the most experienced workman. This apparatus (described on page 211) remained without a serious rival for forty years, and its use has not yet been entirely abandoned.

The next step in advance was the introduction of the expansion pyrometer by John Daniell in 1822. The elongation of a platinum rod, encased in plumbago, was made to operate a magnifying device, which moved a pointer over a scale divided so as to read temperatures directly. Although inaccurate as compared with modern instruments, this pyrometer was the first to give a continuous reading, and required no personal attention. The expansion pyrometer—with different expanding substances—is still used to a limited extent.

The year 1822 was also marked by Seebeck's discovery of thermo-electricity. The generation of a current of electricity by a heated junction of two metals, increasing with the temperature, appeared to afford a simple and satisfactory basis for a pyrometer, and Becquerel constructed an instrument on these lines in 1826. Pouillet and others also endeavoured to measure temperatures by the thermo-electric method, but partly owing to the use of unsuitable junctions, and partly to the lack of reliable galvanometers, these workers failed to obtain concordant results. The method was for all practical purposes abandoned until 1886, when its revival in reliable form led to the enormous extension of the use of pyrometers witnessed during recent years.

In 1828 Prinsep initiated the use of gas pyrometers, and enclosed the gas in a gold bulb. Later workers used porcelain bulbs, on account of greater infusibility, but modern research has shown that porcelain is quite unsuitable for accurate measurements, being porous to certain gases at high temperatures, even when glazed. Gas pyrometers are of little use industrially, but are now used as standards for the calibration of other pyrometers, the bulb being made of an alloy of platinum and rhodium.

Calorimetric pyrometers, based on Regnault's "method of mixtures," were first made for industrial purposes by Byström, who patented an instrument of this type in 1862. This method has been widely applied, and a simplified form of "water" pyrometer, made by Siemens, is at present in daily use for industrial purposes. It is not capable, however, of giving results of the degree of accuracy demanded by many modern processes.

The resistance pyrometer was first described by Sir W. Siemens in 1871, and was made by him for everyday use in furnaces. Many difficulties were encountered before this method was placed on a satisfactory footing, but continuous investigation by the firm of Siemens & Co., and also the valuable researches of Callendar and Griffiths, have resulted in the production of reliable resistance pyrometers, which are extensively used at the present time.

In 1872 Sir William Barrett made a discovery which indirectly led to the present development of the science of pyrometry. Barrett observed that iron and steel, on cooling down from a white heat, suddenly became hotter at a definite point, owing to an internal molecular change; and gave the name of "recalescence" to the phenomenon. Workers in steel subsequently discovered that this property was intimately connected with the hardening of the metal; thus Hadfield noticed that a sample of steel containing 1·16 per cent. of carbon, when quenched just below the change-point was not hardened, but when treated similarly at 15° C. higher it became totally hard. The demand for accurate pyrometers in the steel industry followed immediately on these discoveries, for even the best-trained workman could not detect with the eye a difference in temperature so small, and yet productive of such profound modification of the properties of the finished steel. In this instance, as in many others, the instruments were forthcoming to meet the demand.

The researches of Le Chatelier, published in 1886, marked a great advance in the progress of pyrometry. He discovered that a thermo-electric pyrometer, satisfactory in all respects, could be made by using a junction of pure platinum with a rhodioplatinum alloy, containing 10 per cent. of rhodium; a d'Arsonval moving-coil galvanometer being used as indicator. This type of galvanometer, which permits of an evenly-divided scale, is now universally employed for this purpose, and has made thermo-electric pyrometers not only practicable, but more convenient for general purposes than any other type. Continuous progress has since been made in connection with this method, which is now more extensively used than any other.

Attempts to deduce temperature from the luminosity of the heated body were first made by Ed. Becquerel in 1863, but the method was not successfully developed until 1892, when Le Chatelier introduced his optical pyrometer. This instrument, being entirely external to the hot source, enabled readings to be taken at temperatures far beyond the melting point of platinum, which would obviously be the extreme limit of a pyrometer in which platinum was used. The quantitative distribution of energy in the spectrum has since been worked out by Wien and Planck, who have furnished formula based on thermodynamic reasoning, by the use of which optical pyrometers may now be calibrated in terms of the thermodynamic scale of temperature. Other optical pyrometers, referred to in the text, have been devised by Wanner, Holborn and Kurlbaum, Féry, and others; and the highest attainable temperatures can now be measured satisfactorily by optical means.

The invention of the total-radiation pyrometer by Féry in 1902 added another valuable instrument to those already available. Based on the fourth-power radiation law, discovered by Stefan and confirmed by the mathematical investigations of Boltzmann, this pyrometer is of great service in industrial operations at very high temperatures, being entirely external, and capable of giving permanent records. Modifications have been introduced by Foster and others, and the method is now widely applied.

Recorders, for obtaining permanent evidence of the temperature of a furnace at any time, were first made for thermo-electric pyrometers by Holden and Roberts-Austen, and for resistance pyrometers by Callendar. Numerous forms are now in use, and the value of the records obtained has been abundantly proved.

For scientific purposes, all pyrometers are made to indicate Centigrade degrees, 100 of which represent the temperature interval between the melting-point of ice and the boiling point of water at 760 mm. pressure, the ice-point being marked 0° and the steam-point 100°. In industrial life, however, the Fahrenheit scale is often used in English-speaking countries, the ice-point in this case being numbered 32° and the steam-point 212°; the interval being 180°. A single degree on the Centigrade scale is therefore 1·8 times as large as a Fahrenheit degree, but in finding the numbers on each scale which designate a given temperature, the difference in the zero position on the two scales must be taken into account. When it is desired to translate readings on one scale into the corresponding numbers on the other, the following formula may be used:—

$$\frac{\text{(C. reading)}}{5} = \frac{\text{(F. reading} - 32)}{9}$$

Thus by substituting in the above expression, 660° C. will be found to correspond to 1220° F. and 1530° F. to 832° C.

It is greatly to be regretted that all pyrometers are not made to indicate in Centigrade degrees, as confusion often arises through the use of the two scales. An agreement on this point between instrument makers would overcome the difficulty at once, as the Centigrade scale is now so widely used that few purchasers would insist on Fahrenheit markings.

It may be pointed out here that no single pyrometer is suited to every purpose, and the choice of an instrument must be decided by the nature of the work in hand. A pyrometer requiring skilled attention should not be entrusted to an untrained man; and it may be taken for granted that to obtain the most useful results intelligent supervision is necessary. In the ensuing pages the advantages and drawbacks of each type will be considered; but in all cases it is desirable, before making any large outlay on pyrometers, to obtain a competent and impartial opinion as to the kind best suited to the processes to be controlled. Catalogue descriptions are not always trustworthy, and instances are not wanting in which a large sum has been expended on instruments which, owing to wrong choice, have proved practically useless. An instrument suited to laboratory measurements is often a failure in the workshop, and all possibilities of this kind should be considered before deciding upon the type of pyrometer to be used.

CHAPTER II
STANDARDS OF TEMPERATURE

The Absolute or Thermodynamic Scale of Temperatures.—
All practical instruments for measuring temperatures are based on some progressive physical change on the part of a substance or substances. In a mercury thermometer, the alteration in the volume of the liquid is used as a measure of hotness; and similarly the change in volume or pressure on the part of a gas, or the variation in resistance to electricity shown by a metal, and many other physical changes, may be employed for this purpose. In connection with the measurement of high temperatures, many different physical principles are relied upon in the various instruments in use, and it is of the greatest importance that all should read alike under the same conditions. This result would not be attained if each instrument were judged by its own performances. In the case of a mercury thermometer, for example, we may indicate the amount of expansion between the temperatures of ice and steam at 76 centimetres pressure, representing 100° Centigrade, by a; and then assume that an expansion of $2a$ will signify a temperature of 200°, and so on in proportion. Similarly, we may find the increase in resistance manifested by platinum between the same two fixed points, and indicate it by r, and then assume that an increase of $2r$ will correspond to 200°. If now we compare the two instruments, we find that they do not agree, for on placing both in a space in which the platinum instrument registered 200°, the mercury thermometer would show 203°. A similar, or even greater, discrepancy would be observed if other physical changes were relied upon to furnish temperature scales on these lines, and it is therefore highly desirable that a standard independent of any physical property of matter should be used. Such a standard is to be found in the thermodynamic scale of temperatures, originally suggested by Lord Kelvin. This scale is based upon the conversion of heat into work in a heat engine, a process which is independent of the nature of the medium used. A temperature scale founded on this conversion is therefore not connected with any physical property of matter, and furnishes a standard of reference to which all practical appliances for measuring temperatures may be

compared.[1] When readings are expressed in terms of this scale, it is customary to use the letter K in conjunction with the number: thus 850° K would mean 850 degrees on the thermodynamic scale.

When existing instruments are compared with this standard, it is found that a scale based on the assumption that the volume of a gas free to expand, or the pressure of a confined gas, increases directly as the temperature is in close agreement with the thermodynamic scale. It may be proved that if the gas employed were "perfect," a scale in exact conformity with the standard described would be secured; and gases which approach nearest in properties to a perfect gas, such as hydrogen, nitrogen, and air, may therefore be used to produce a practical standard, the indications of which are nearly identical with the thermodynamic scale. If any other physical change be chosen, such as the expansion of a solid, or the increase in resistance of a metal, and a temperature scale be based on the supposition that the change in question varies directly as the temperature, the results obtained would differ considerably from the absolute standard. For this reason the practical standard of temperature now universally adopted is an instrument based on the properties of a suitable gas.

The Constant Volume Gas Thermometer.—In applying the properties of a gas to practical temperature measurement, we may devise some means of determining the increase in volume when the gas is allowed to expand, or the increase in pressure of a confined gas may be observed. The latter procedure is more convenient in practice, and the instrument used for this purpose is known as the constant volume gas thermometer, one form of which is shown in fig. 1. The gas is enclosed in a bulb B, connected to a tube bent into a parallel branch, into the bend of which is sealed a tap C, furnished with a drying cup. The extremity of the parallel branch is connected to a piece of flexible tubing T, which communicates with a mercury cistern which may be moved over a scale, the rod G serving as a guide. In using this instrument the bulb B is immersed in ice, and the tap C opened. When the temperature has fallen to 0° C., the mercury is brought to the mark A by adjusting the cistern, and the tap C then closed. The bulb B is now placed in the space or medium of which the temperature is to be determined, and expansion prevented by raising the cistern so as to keep the mercury at A. When steady, the height of the mercury in the cistern above the level of A is read off, and furnishes a clue to the temperature of B. If the coefficient of pressure of the gas used (in this case, air) be known, the temperature may be calculated from the equation

$$P_1 = P_0(1 + bt),$$

where P_1 is the pressure at $t°$; P_0 the pressure at $0°$; and b the coefficient of pressure; that is, the increase in unit pressure at $0°$ for a rise in temperature of $1°$. Thus if $P_0 = 76$ cms.; $b = 0.00367$; height of mercury in cistern above $A = 55.8$ cms.; then

$$P_1 = (76 + 55.8) = 131.8 \text{ cms.},$$

and by inserting these values in the above equation t is found to be $200°$. In the instrument described, P_0 is equal to the height of the barometer, since the tap C is open whilst the bulb is immersed in ice. The coefficient of pressure may be determined by placing the bulb in steam at a known temperature, and noting the increased pressure. In the equation given, P_1, P_0, and t are then known, and the value of b may be calculated.

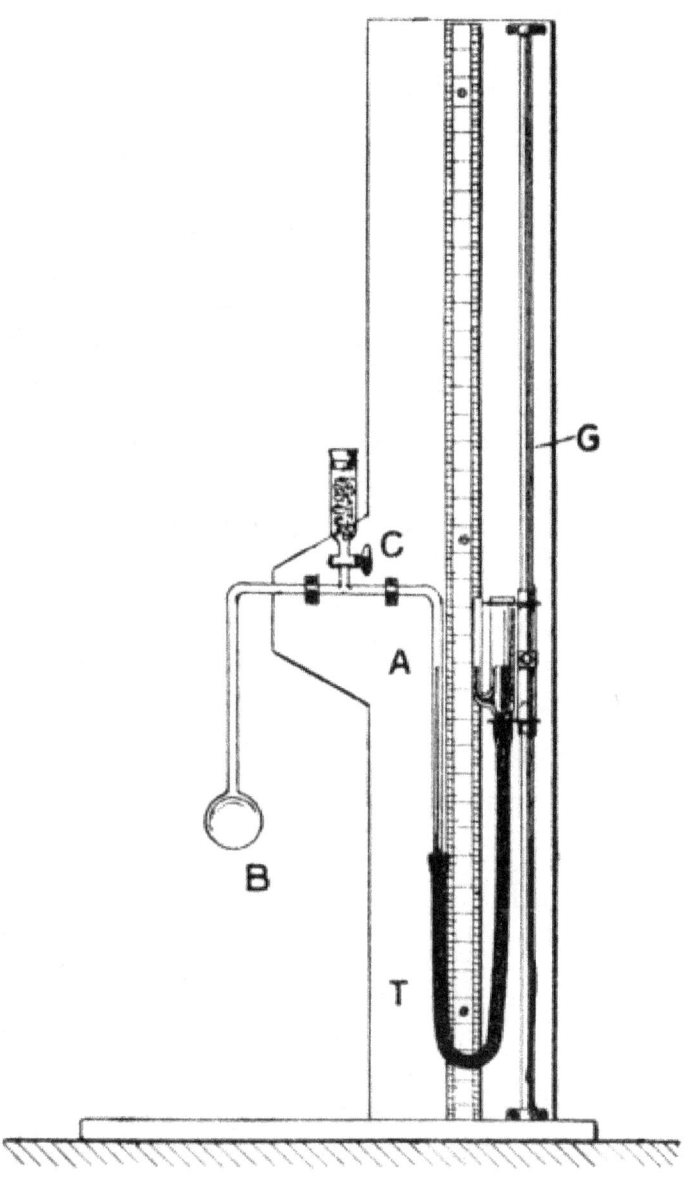

Fig. 1.—Constant Volume Air Thermometer.

In using this instrument for exact determinations of temperature, allowance must be made for the expansion of the bulb, which causes a lower pressure to be registered than would be noted if the bulb were non-expansive. Again, the gas in the connecting tube is not at the same temperature as that in the bulb; an error which may be practically eliminated by making the bulb large and the bore of the tube small. The temperature of the mercury column must also be allowed for, as the density varies with the temperature. When the various corrections have been made, readings of great accuracy may be secured.

When applied to the measurement of high temperatures, the bulb must be made of a more infusible material than glass. Gold, porcelain, platinum, and quartz have been used by different investigators, but the most reliable material for temperatures exceeding 900° C. has been found to be an alloy of platinum with 20 per cent. of rhodium. The most suitable gas to use inside the bulb is nitrogen, which is chemically inert towards the materials of the bulb, and is not absorbed by the metals mechanically. When measuring high temperatures with this instrument, a considerable pressure, amounting to 1 atmosphere for every increase of 273 degrees above the ice point, is requisite to prevent expansion of the nitrogen; and this pressure tends to distort the bulb and so to falsify the indications. This trouble has been overcome by Day, who surrounded the bulb by a second larger bulb, and forced air or nitrogen into the intervening space until the pressure on the exterior of the thermometer bulb was equal to that prevailing in the interior. Even then it was not found possible to secure higher readings than 1550° C., as the bulb commenced to alter in shape owing to the softening of the material. This temperature represents the highest yet measured on the gas scale; but by using a more refractory material, such as fused zirconia, it may be found possible to extend this range to 2000° C. or more. Experiments in this direction are very desirable, in order that high-reading pyrometers may be checked directly against the gas scale.

Fixed Points for Calibration of Pyrometers.—It is evident that the gas thermometer is totally unsuited for use in workshops or laboratories when a rapid determination of a high temperature is required. Its function is to establish fixed points or temperature standards, by means of which other instruments, more convenient to use, may be graduated so as to agree with each other and with the gas scale itself. The temperature scales of all modern pyrometers are thus derived, directly or indirectly, from the gas thermometer. In the table on next page, a number of fixed points, determined by various observers, is given; the error, even at the highest temperatures, probably not exceeding ±2° C.

In preparing the temperature scale of a pyrometer for practical use, the instrument is subjected successively to a number of the temperatures indicated in the table, and in this manner several fixed points are established on its scale. The space between these points is then suitably subdivided to represent intermediate temperatures.

Table of Fixed Points.

Substance.	Physical Condition.	Deg. Cent.	Deg. Fahr.
Water (ice)	At Melting Point	0	32
Water	” Boiling ”	100	212
Aniline	” ” ”	184	363
Naphthalene	” ” ”	218	424
Tin	” Melting ”	232	449
Lead	” ” ”	327	620
Zinc	” ” ”	419	786
Sulphur	” Boiling ”	445	833
Antimony	” Melting ”	631	1167
Aluminium	” ” ”	657	1214
Common Salt	” ” ”	800	1472
Silver (in air)	” ” ”	955	1751
Silver (free from oxygen)	” ” ”	962	1763
Gold	” ” ”	1064	1947
Copper (in air)	” ” ”	1064	1947
Copper (Graphite covered)	” ” ”	1084	1983
Iron (pure)	” ” ”	1520	2768
Palladium	” ” ”	1549	2820
Platinum	” ” ”	1755	3190

It is necessary to point out that the figures given in the table refer only to pure substances, and that relatively small quantities of impurities may give rise to serious errors. The methods by which the physical condition to which the temperatures refer may be realised in practice will be described in the succeeding chapter.

National Physical Laboratory Scale.—Exact agreement with regard to fixed points has not yet been arrived at in different countries, and an effort to co-ordinate the work of the National Physical Laboratory, the United States Bureau of Standards, and the Reichsanstalt, with a view to the formation of an international scale, was interrupted by the war. In 1916 the National Physical Laboratory adopted a set of fixed points on the Centigrade thermodynamic scale, in conformity with which all British pyrometers have since been standardised. It will be seen that the figures differ very slightly from those given in the previous table, which represent the average results of separate determinations in different countries.

NATIONAL PHYSICAL LABORATORY SCALE (1916)

Substance.	Physical Condition.	Deg. Cent.	Deg. Fahr.
Water (ice)	At Melting Point	0	32
Water	" Boiling " (760 mm.)	100	212
Naphthalene	" " " "	217·9	424
Benzophenone	" " " "	305·9	582
Zinc	At Melting Point	419·4	787
Antimony	" " "	630	1166
Common Salt	" " "	801	1474
Silver (in reducing atmosphere)	" " "	961	1761
Gold	" " "	1063	1945
Copper (in reducing atmosphere)	" " "	1083	1982

For higher temperatures the melting points of nickel (1452° C.) and palladium (1549° C.) are employed, but the accuracy in these cases is not so certain as with the substances named in the table. A useful point, intermediate between copper and nickel, has been established by E. Griffiths, and is obtained by heating nickel with an excess of graphite, when a well-defined eutectic is formed which freezes at 1330° C., or 2426° F.

Temperatures above the Present Limit of the Gas Thermometer.—As it is not yet possible to compare an instrument directly with the gas thermometer above 1550° C., all higher temperatures must be arrived at by a process of extrapolation. By careful observation of a physical change at temperatures up to the limit of 1550° C., the law governing such change may be discovered; and assuming the law to hold indefinitely, higher temperatures may be deduced by calculation. An amount of uncertainty always attaches to this procedure, and in the past some ludicrous figures have been given as the result of indefinite extrapolation. Wedgwood, for example, by assuming the uniform contraction of clay, gave 12001° C., or 21637° F., as the melting point of wrought iron, whereas the correct figure is 1520° C., according to the gas scale. Even in recent times, the extrapolation of the law connecting the temperature of a thermal junction with the electromotive force developed, obtained by comparison with the gas scale up to 1100° C., led Harker to the conclusion that the melting point of platinum was 1710° C., a figure 45 degrees lower than that now accepted. The laws governing the radiation of energy at different temperatures, however, appear to be capable of mathematical proof from thermodynamic principles, and temperatures derived from these laws are in reality expressed on the absolute or thermodynamic scale. Extrapolation of these laws, when used to deduce temperatures by means of radiation pyrometers, appears to be justified; but it is still desirable to extend the gas scale as far as possible to check such instruments. Assuming the radiation laws to hold, it is possible to determine the highest temperatures procurable, such as that of the electric arc, with a reasonable degree of certainty.

[1] For a fuller account of the thermodynamic scale, see the author's treatise *HeatforEngineers* , pp. 391-2.

CHAPTER III
THERMO-ELECTRIC PYROMETERS

General Principles.—Seebeck, in 1822, made the discovery that when a junction of two dissimilar metals is heated an electromotive force is set up at the junction, which gives rise to a current of electricity when the heated junction forms part of a closed circuit. Becquerel, in 1826, attempted to apply this discovery to the measurement of high temperatures, it having been observed that in general the E.M.F. increased as the temperature of the junction was raised. No concordant results were obtained, and the same fate befell the investigations of others who subsequently attempted to produce pyrometers based on the Seebeck effect. These failures were due to several causes, but chiefly to the non-existence of reliable galvanometers, such as we now possess. It was not until 1886 that the problem was satisfactorily solved by Le Chatelier of Paris.

Although any heated junction of metals will give rise to an electromotive force, it does not follow that any pair, taken at random, will be suited to the purposes of a pyrometer. A junction of iron and copper, for example, gives rise to an E.M.F. which increases with the temperature up to a certain point, beyond which the E.M.F. falls off although the temperature rises, and finally reverses in direction—a phenomenon to which the name of "thermo-electric inversion" has been applied. Evidently, it would be impossible to measure temperatures in this case from observations of the electromotive force produced, and any couple chosen must be free from this deterrent property. Moreover, the metals used must not undergo deterioration, or alteration in thermo-electric properties, when subjected for a prolonged period to the temperature it is desired to measure. These and other considerations greatly restrict the choice of a suitable pair of metals, which, to give satisfaction, should conform to the following conditions:—

1. The E.M.F. developed by the junction should increase uniformly as the temperature rises.

2. The melting point of either component should be well above the highest temperature to be measured. An exception to this rule occurs when the E.M.F. of fused materials is employed.

3. The thermo-electric value of the couple should not be altered by prolonged heating.

4. The metals should be capable of being drawn into homogeneous wires, so that a junction, wherever formed, may always give rise to the same E.M.F. under given conditions.

It is a further advantage if the metals which fulfil the above conditions are cheap and durable.

The exacting character of these requirements delayed the production of a reliable thermo-electric pyrometer until 1886, when Le Chatelier discovered that a junction formed of platinum as one metal, and an alloy of 90 per cent. of platinum and 10 per cent. of rhodium as the other, gave concordant results. In measuring the E.M.F. produced, Le Chatelier took advantage of the moving-coil galvanometer introduced by d'Arsonval, which possessed the advantages of an evenly-divided scale and a dead-beat action. This happy combination of a suitable junction with a simple and satisfactory indicator immediately established the reliability of the thermo-electric method of measuring temperatures. As platinum melts at 1755° C., and the rhodium alloy at a still higher temperature, a means was thus provided of controlling most of the industrial operations carried out in furnaces.

So far, the effect of heating the junction has been considered without regard to the temperature of the remainder of the circuit, and it is necessary, before describing the construction of practical instruments, to consider the laws governing the thermo-electric circuit, the simplest form of which is represented in [fig. 2](). One of the wires is connected at both ends to separate pieces of the other wire, the free ends of which are taken to the galvanometer Two junctions, A and B, are thus formed, which evidently act in opposition; for if on heating A the direction of current be from A to B, then on heating B the direction will be from B to A. Hence if A and B were equally heated no current would flow in the circuit, the arrangement being equivalent to two cells of equal E.M.F. in opposition. Thermal junctions are formed at each of the galvanometer terminals, but the currents to which they give rise, when the temperature changes, are opposed and cancel each other. The law which holds for this circuit may be expressed thus:—

> "If in a thermo-electric circuit there be two junctions, A and B, the electromotive force developed is proportional to the *difference* in temperature between A and B."

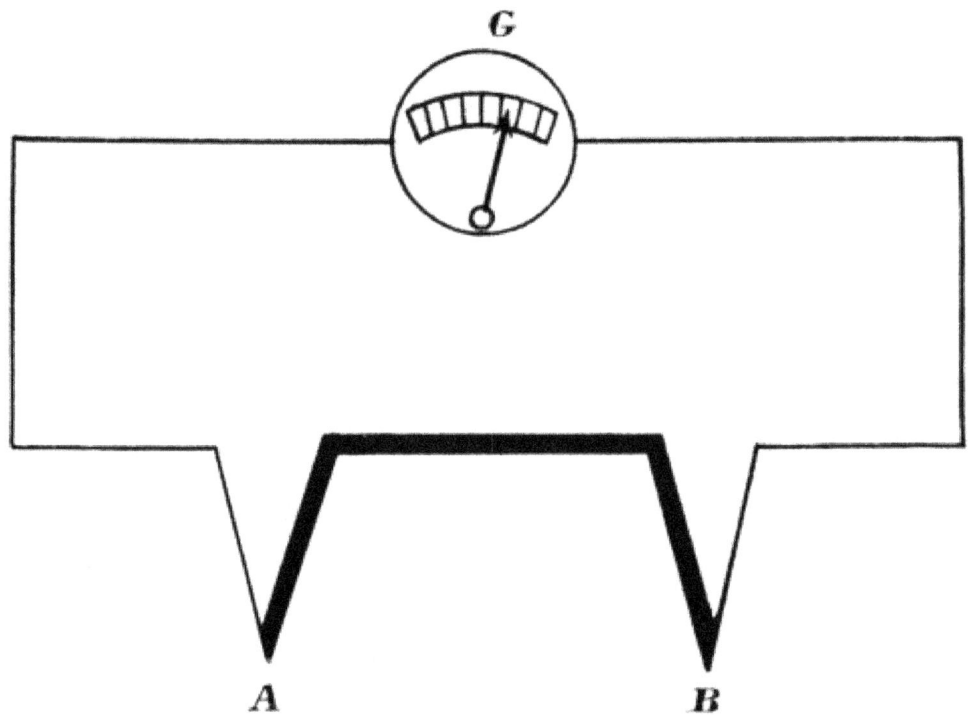

FIG. 2.—TWO-JUNCTION THERMO-ELECTRIC CIRCUIT.

It is customary to refer to the two junctions as the "hot" and "cold" junctions; but it is important to remember that fluctuations in the temperature of either will alter the reading on the galvanometer or indicator.

A second law, which applies to all thermo-electric circuits, is that "the E.M.F. developed is independent of the thickness of the wire." This does not mean that the deflection of the galvanometer is the same whether thin or thick wires are used to form the junction. The deflection depends upon the current flowing through the circuit, and this, according to Ohm's law, varies inversely as the total resistance of the circuit. Consequently, the use of thin wires of a given kind will tend to give a less deflection than in the case of thick wires, as the resistance of the former will be greater, and unless the resistance of the galvanometer be great compared with that of the junction, the difference in deflection will be conspicuous. The E.M.F., however, is the same under given conditions, whatever thickness of wire be used.

Reference to fig. 2 will show that in order to realise this circuit in practice, one of the wires forming the couple must be used in the form of leads to the galvanometer. This can readily be done if the material of the wire is cheap; but if platinum or other expensive metal be used, and the galvanometer be some yards distant, the question of cost necessitates a compromise, and the circuit is then arranged as in fig. 3. The wires forming the hot junction are brought to brass terminals T T, from which copper wires lead to the galvanometer G. This arrangement results in three effective junctions, viz. the hot junction A to B; the junction A to brass, and the junction B to brass. It will be seen that the two junctions of copper to brass are in opposition, and cancel each other for equal heating; and the same applies to the galvanometer connections. A circuit thus composed of three separate junctions does not permit of a simple expression for the net E.M.F. under varying temperature conditions, and to avoid errors in readings care must be taken to prevent any notable change of temperature at the terminals T T in a practical instrument arranged as in the diagram.

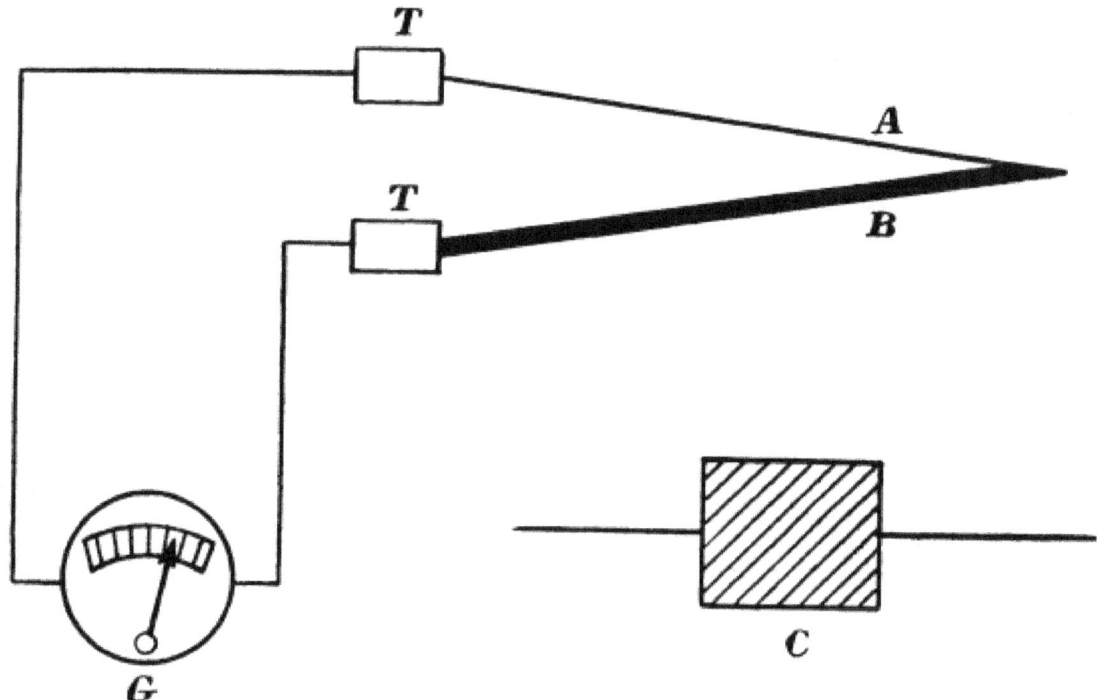

FIG. 3.—THREE-JUNCTION THERMO-ELECTRIC CIRCUIT.

A point of practical utility in thermo-electric work is the fact that if a wire be interrupted by a length of other metal, as indicated at C in fig. 3, no current will be set up in a circuit if both joints are equally heated, as the electromotive forces generated at each junction are in opposition. It is thus possible to interrupt a circuit by a plug-key or switch, without introducing an error; always provided that an even temperature prevails over the region containing the joints.

Another useful fact is that if two wires be brought into contact, they may be fastened over the joint by soldering or using a third metal, without alteration of thermo-electric value, except in rare cases. Thus a copper-constantan or iron-constantan junction may suitably be united by silver solder, using borax as a flux, thus avoiding the uncertainty of contact which must always occur when the wires are merely twisted together. Welding, however, is preferable to soldering.

Metals used for Thermal Junctions.—Until recent years it was customary to employ a platinum-rhodioplatinum or platinum-iridioplatinum junction for all temperatures beyond the scope of the mercury thermometer. The almost prohibitive price of these metals has caused investigations to be made with a view to discovering cheaper substitutes, with successful results up to 1000° C. or 1800° F., thus comprehending the range of temperatures employed in many industrial processes. Above this temperature the platinum series of metals are still used for accurate working, but it will be of great advantage if the range measurable by cheap or "base" metals can be further extended. Promise in this direction is afforded by the properties of fused metals when used in thermal junctions. An investigation by the author has shown that in general the E.M.F. developed by a junction does not undergo any sudden change when one or both metals melt, but continues as if fusion had not occurred. By making arrangements to maintain the continuity of the circuit after fusion, it may be possible to read temperatures approximating to the boiling points of metals such as copper and tin, both of which are over 2000° C. The base metals are not so durable as platinum and kindred metals, but as the cost of replacement is negligible, this drawback is of little importance. Moreover, base-metal junctions usually develop a much higher E.M.F. than the platinum metals, which enables stronger and cheaper galvanometers to be used as indicators.

THERMAL JUNCTIONS USED IN PYROMETERS.

Couple.	Upper limit to which Junction may be used.	
	Deg. Cent.	Deg. Fahr.
Platinum and rhodioplatinum (10 per cent. Rh)	1400	2550
2 Rhodioplatinum alloys of different composition	1600	2900
Platinum and iridioplatinum (10 per cent. Ir)	1100	2000
Nickel and constantan	900	1650
Nickel and copper	800	1475
Nickel and carbon	1000	1850
Nickel and iron	1000	1850
Iron and constantan	900	1650
Copper and constantan	800	1475
Silver and constantan	800	1475
2 Nickel chrome alloys of different composition (Hoskin's alloys)	1100	2010
Nickel-chrome alloy and nickel-aluminium alloy	1100	2010
2 Iron-nickel alloys of different composition	1000	1850

The electromotive force developed by a junction of any given pair of metals when heated to a given temperature varies according to the origin of the metals. It is not unusual, for example, for two samples of 10 per cent. rhodioplatinum, obtained from different sources, to show a difference in this respect of 40 per cent. when coupled with the same piece of platinum. Equal or greater divergences may be noted with other metals; and hence the replacement of a junction can only be effected, with accuracy, by wires from the same lengths of which the junction formed a part. As showing how platinum itself is not uniform, it may be mentioned that almost any two pieces of platinum wire, if not from the same length, will cause a deflection on a sensitive galvanometer when made into a junction and heated. It is therefore customary for makers to obtain considerable quantities of wire of a given kind, homogeneous as far as possible, in order that a number of identical instruments may be made, and the junctions replaced, when necessary, without alteration of the scale of the indicator.

The alloy known as "constantan," which figures largely in the foregoing table, is composed of nickel and copper, and is practically identical with the alloy sold as "Eureka" or "Advance." It has a high specific resistance, and a very small temperature coefficient, and is much used for winding resistances. Couples formed of constantan and other metals furnish on heating an E.M.F. several times greater than that yielded by couples of the platinum series, and show an equally steady rise of E.M.F. with temperature. This alloy has proved of great service in connection with the thermo-electric method of measuring temperatures. Couples formed of nickel-chrome alloys, known as "Hoskin's alloys," have been introduced into Britain by the Foster Instrument Company, which may be used continuously to 1100° C., and for occasional readings up to 1300° C. Another couple, much used in America, consists of an alloy of 90 per cent. nickel and 10 per cent. chromium, and an alloy of 98 per cent. nickel and 2 per cent. aluminium, which may be used up to 1100° C. Other couples, formed of alloys of nickel, chromium, iron, aluminium, etc., have been introduced by different makers, but have not proved so satisfactory as those mentioned above.

Changes in Thermal Junctions when constantly used.—No metal appears to be able to withstand a high temperature continuously without undergoing some physical alteration; and for this reason the E.M.F. developed by a given junction is liable to change after a period of constant use. At temperatures above 1100° C., platinum, for example, undergoes a notable change in a comparatively short period, but below 1000° C., the change is very slight, and if this range be not exceeded, a platinum-rhodioplatinum or iridioplatinum junction may be used for years without serious error arising from this cause. This liability to change is one of the factors which restricts the range of thermal junctions, which should never be used continuously beyond the temperature at which the alteration commences to become large. A second cause of discrepancy is the possible alteration in the composition of an alloy, due to one of the constituents leaving in the form of vapour, as is noted with iridioplatinum alloys, from which the iridium volatilises in tangible quantities above 1100° C., causing a fall of 10 per cent. or more in the thermo-electric value of the junction of these alloys with platinum. Constantan appears to be very stable in its thermo-electric properties, and the various junctions in which it plays a part show a high degree of stability if not overheated. Rhodioplatinum alloys are very stable, and for temperatures exceeding 1100° C. a junction of two of these alloys, of different composition, is more durable than one in which pure platinum is used. An extended series of tests on base-metal junctions made in America by Kowalke showed that continuous heating of couples as received from the makers altered the E.M.F. considerably, the change in some cases representing over 100° C. on the indicator. A stable condition, due to the relief of strains or other change, was finally reached, and the conclusion drawn that the materials should be thoroughly annealed before calibration. It is desirable in all cases periodically to test the junctions at some standard temperature, and if any conspicuous error be noted, to replace the old junction by a new one.

In addition to the errors due to slow physical changes, a junction may be altered considerably, if imperfectly protected, owing to the chemical action of furnace gases, or of solids with which the junction may come into contact. The vapours of metals such as lead or antimony are very injurious; and platinum in particular is seriously affected by vapours containing phosphorus, if in a reducing atmosphere. So searching is the corrosive action of furnace gases that adequate protection of the junction is essential if errors and damage are to be avoided. When a wire has once been corroded, a junction made with it will not develop the same E.M.F. as before.

Electromotive Force developed by Typical Junctions.—The following table exhibits the E.M.F. generated by several junctions for a range of 100° C., taken at the middle part of the working range in each case. These figures are subject to considerable variation, according to the origin of the metals.

Couple.	E.M.F. in millivolts for a rise of 100° at middle of working range.
Platinum-rhodioplatinum (10 per cent. Rh)	1·1
Platinum-iridioplatinum (10 per cent. Ir)	1·2

Nickel-constantan	2·3
Copper-constantan	5·8
Nickel-copper	6·1
Iron-constantan	6·7
Hoskin's alloys	7·4

It will be noted that the base-metal junctions give much higher values than the platinum series, and hence can be used with a less sensitive, and therefore cheaper, indicator. Base-metal junctions are also, in consequence of the greater E.M.F. furnished, capable of yielding more sensitive readings over a selected range of temperature.

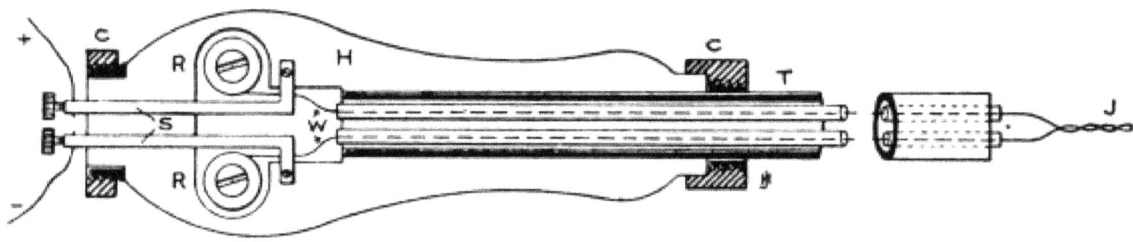

FIG. 4.—PRACTICAL FORM OF THERMO-ELECTRIC PYROMETER.

Practical Forms of Thermocouples.—When expensive junctions are employed, wires of the minimum thickness consistent with strength and convenience of construction are used, a diameter of No. 25 standard wire gauge being suitable. A common arrangement is shown in fig. 4, in which J is the hot junction, the wires from which are passed through thin fireclay tubes which serve as insulators (or through twin-bore fireclay) to the reels R R, in the head of the pyrometer, upon which a quantity of spare wire is wound to enable new junctions to be made when required. Two brass strips, S, are screwed down on to the wires at one end, and are furnished with screw terminals at the other end, from which wires are taken to the galvanometer or indicator. A protecting-tube, T, surrounds the wires and hot junction. The head, H, may be constructed of wood, fibre, or porcelain, and should be an insulator for electricity and heat. There are various modifications in use, but the general method described is adopted by most makers. In order to guard against errors arising from alterations in the temperature of the cold junctions in the end of the pyrometer, some firms construct the head so as to leave a hollow space, through which cold water is constantly circulated (fig. 5), the arrangement being known as a "water-cooled head." In some forms the supply of spare wires is made to take the form of two spiral springs in a hollow head, the upper ends of the springs being taken to terminals.

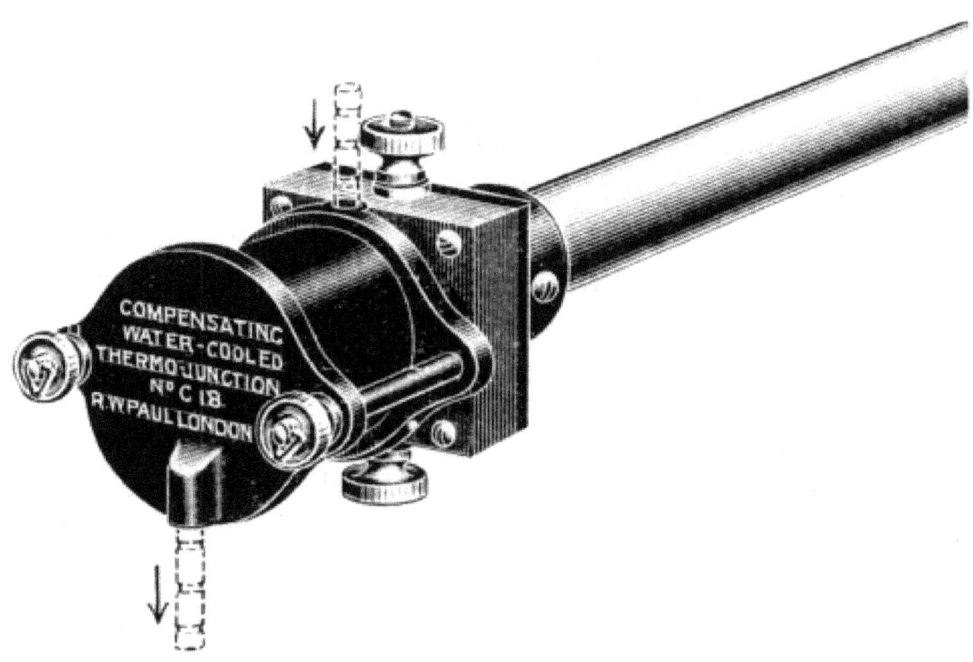

FIG. 5.—PYROMETER WITH WATER-COOLED HEAD.

The choice of a protecting-tube is a matter of considerable importance. Obviously, such a tube should not soften at the highest temperature attained, and when expensive metals are used to form the junction the sheath should not be permeable to gases or vapours. It should also, if possible, be a good conductor of heat, so that the junction may respond quickly to a change of temperature in its surroundings, and should be mechanically strong. It is difficult to secure all these properties in any single material, and the choice of a sheath is decided by the conditions under which the couple is to be used. The substances employed, and their properties and special uses, may be enumerated as follows:—

1. *Iron or Mild Steel.*—For temperatures not exceeding 1100° C. iron or mild steel covers are cheap and efficient from the standpoint of conductivity, although liable to deteriorate owing to oxidation. The tendency to oxidise is greatly diminished by "calorising" the exterior by Ruder's process, in which the iron is heated in a mixture of metallic aluminium and oxide of aluminium, a surface alloy being formed which

resists oxidation. A result nearly as good may be obtained by smearing the surface with fine aluminium powder, and bringing to a white heat. This treatment greatly prolongs the life of an iron sheath. Some makers employ an inner steel tube round the wires, and an outer tube which comes into contact with the furnace gases, corrosion of the latter being detected before the inner tube has given way and exposed the junction. Some makers do not consider it safe to expose heated platinum to an iron surface, with only air intervening, and hence use an inner cover of silica or porcelain, which the outer iron or steel tube protects from mechanical damage. For ordinary work seamless steam or hydraulic steel tubing, with a welded end, is satisfactory; but for dipping into molten lead or other metals the tube should be bored from the solid. The great advantage of an iron or steel sheath is its mechanical strength, which protects the couple from damage in case of rough usage.

2. *Nichrom.*—Certain alloys of nickel and chromium, and especially that known as Nichrom II, may be kept at 1100° C. without oxidising to any appreciable extent; and hence sheaths of this material may be used up to the temperature named. In addition to being more durable than iron, nichrom possesses the same advantages of strength and good conductivity; on the other hand, it is more costly.

3. *Molybdenum.*—This metal, which possesses a melting point of about 2500° C., may be dipped in molten brass, bronze, copper, etc., without being attacked, and has been used to form the tip of a protecting-tube designed to measure the temperature of molten alloys. A junction covered only by a thin tube of molybdenum quickly attains the temperature of its surroundings.

4. *Graphite and Graphite Compositions.*—Carbon has the highest melting point of all known substances, and in the form of artificial or Acheson graphite may be easily machined to any desired shape. Graphite sheaths are sometimes used for immersion in molten metals, but at 1000° C. and higher Acheson graphite oxidises easily and becomes friable. It is a good conductor of heat, but is easily broken. Compositions of natural graphite and refractory earths, such as Morgan's "Salamander," are inferior to pure graphite in conductivity, but are stronger and not readily oxidised, and may be used to form sheaths for temperatures up to 1400° C. or

possibly higher, when penetration of furnace gases to the junction is not of moment.

5. *Porcelain.*—This material, in its best forms, may be used up to 1400° C., but must be efficiently glazed to prevent the ingress of furnace gases to the junction. It is easily broken by a blow, and when circumstances permit should be protected by an iron covering-sheath. The variety known as "Marquardt" has been found very satisfactory for high-reading thermal couples. Porcelain is not a good conductor of heat, and a junction encased in it does not respond quickly to external changes in temperature.

6. *Vitrified Silica.*—This substance, which may be worked in the oxy-hydrogen blowpipe, is largely used as a protecting-tube. It is not advisable, however, to use it for continuous work above 1100° C., as beyond this temperature devitrification occurs, and the tube becomes porous. It is a fairly good conductor of heat, and withstands rapid changes in temperature without cracking. It is very brittle, and for this reason is generally encased in iron.

7. *Alundum.*—This material is made from fused bauxite, and has a melting point of 2050° C. A special form of alundum, used for protecting-tubes, is non-porous up to 1300° C., and forms a satisfactory covering. Alundum is a moderately good conductor of heat, but is easily broken.

8. *Carborundum.*—This is an electric furnace product, which may be heated above 2000° C. without damage. For making into pyrometer tubes, it is bonded with a suitable material, and baked after shaping. Carborundum, and the amorphous variety known as "silfrax," have proved useful for protecting junctions at temperatures as high as 1600° C. The thermal conductivity is relatively good, but the tubes are easily broken.

9. *Magnesia.*—Tubes of this material, which melts at a temperature considerably above 2000° C., have been used for special work. Magnesia is a poor conductor of heat, and has little mechanical strength.

10. *Zirconia.*—This is a very refractory material, its melting point exceeding 2500° C. It may be made into a vitreous variety, which is non-porous and proof against sudden temperature changes. At present, only a moulded form of pyrometer tube, made from zirconia powder, is available, the material worked in this manner being termed "zirkite." Although

zirconia is a bad conductor of heat, its other qualities are such that it forms an excellent material for work at the highest temperatures possible for thermal junctions; and when the vitreous variety is available, may come into extended use.

Fig. 6.
Pyrometer
with
Special
Cold
Junction
in Head.

It will be seen from the foregoing that the ideal protecting-tube has yet to be found, and the user must choose the one which comes nearest to his requirements. Special consideration must be given in cases when chemical fumes are present, and a sheath selected which is not attacked or penetrated by them.

Returning to the junction, it is advisable always to weld the wires, and not to rely upon the contact resulting from twisting them together. Platinum and the platinum alloys may be welded readily by placing the junction in a coal-gas blowpipe fed with oxygen instead of air. For work at lower temperatures the platinum metals may be soldered by means of a small quantity of gold, in the flame of a Bunsen burner.

When cheap metals are used for the junction the construction may be considerably modified, and often with advantage. In fig. 6, for example, which represents a thermocouple made by A. Gallenkamp & Co., the metals used are copper and constantan, and the hot junction, fastened by silver solder, is supplemented by a cold junction of the same metals located in the head. The copper wire from the hot junction passes directly to a copper terminal, from whence a copper wire lead is carried to the galvanometer; and the same procedure is carried out with the copper wire from the cold junction, thus realising the circuit shown in fig. 2. The cold junction is kept in oil, the temperature of which is registered by a short thermometer, thus enabling (as will be explained later) the correct temperature of the hot junction to be deduced under any circumstances. In this instrument twin-bore fireclay is used to insulate the wires, and the protecting-tube is of iron —which suffices for the upper limit (800° C.) to which the junction may be used. Iron and constantan could be used in this manner by employing iron leads to the galvanometer.

Another type of instrument, rendered practicable by the use of cheap metals, and which may be termed the "heavy type," is constructed of thick pieces of the metals welded together instead of wires, thus ensuring greater strength and longer life. Messrs Crompton & Co. were the first to introduce thermocouples of this type, consisting of a heavy steel tube, to one end of which a nickel rod is welded, the other end being free, and the length of the rod suitably insulated from the steel tube; leads for the rod and tube being taken to the galvanometer. Fig. 7 shows a couple of this kind, made by Paul, consisting of an iron tube down the middle of which a constantan rod is passed, insulated from the tube by magnesia. At the tapered end the two metals are welded together, and at the free end a special cap, fitted over the tube and rod, the contact parts being insulated from one another, serves to enable leads to be taken to the galvanometer. Similar thermocouples are made by the Foster Instrument Company (fig. 8), and are simple, cheap, and reliable up to 900° C. with an iron-constantan couple, and to 1100° C. with nichrom couples. When worn out they may be replaced, at a trifling cost, by others made from the same batch of metal.

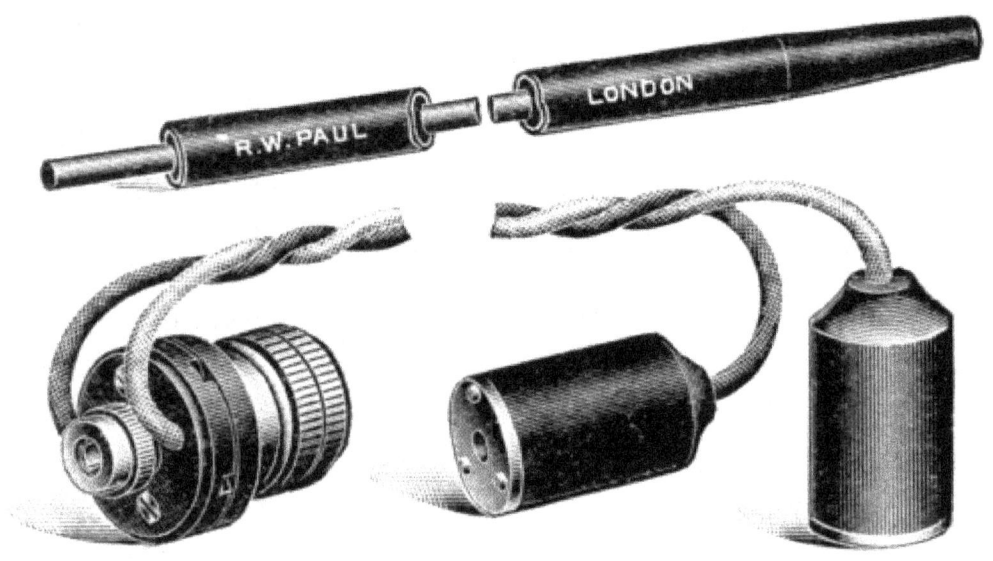

Fig. 7.—Heavy Type, Cheap-metal Pyrometer.

The drawback to the use of carbon as one of the materials for a junction is the difficulty experienced in securing a good contact with the metal with which it is coupled. In nickel-carbon junctions the contact is sometimes ensured by the aid of a spring, which presses the two substances together. Such an arrangement is evidently not so reliable as one in which the materials are welded, and a defective contact, arising from any cause, would lead to serious error. A preferable plan is to screw both the nickel and carbon rods into a cross-piece of either element.

FIG. 8.—FOSTER'S CHEAP-METAL PYROMETER.

When applying a thermal junction to the measurement of surface temperatures, such as steam-pipes or the exterior of furnaces, the wires may be passed through a thin disc of metal, about ¼ in. in diameter, and soldered at the back. Suitable materials are copper and constantan, soldered to a thin copper disc with silver solder, and brought to a cold junction in the head of the instrument as shown in fig. 6. The terminal piece of the insulation may be made of hard wood, with the holes countersunk so as to cover the solder and enable the wood to touch the disc, which, when pressed on the hot surface, will then rapidly acquire the temperature. The author has found, by trials under varying circumstances, that this method of measuring surface temperatures gives reliable and concordant results. For very high surface temperatures a platinum disc, with one of the usual platinum metal couples soldered to the disc with pure silver, and a piece of twin-bore fireclay brought to the back of the disc, will be found to suffice for most cases arising in practice. A small blowpipe flame is best for soldering the wires to the disc, borax being used as flux in the first case; but no flux is necessary in soldering the platinum metals with pure silver.

In deciding upon the length of a thermocouple it must be remembered that the temperature recorded is that prevailing in the region of the hot junction. When the temperature of a furnace is uniform it is sufficient to allow the end of the thermocouple to protrude about 12 inches into the interior, but when following the change of temperature undergone by objects in a furnace the end must be located near the objects. If the distance from the exterior of the furnace to the objects exceed 2 feet, the thermocouple should be inserted through the roof so as to hang vertically, as if placed through the side it would droop by its own weight at high temperatures. The distance between the exterior of the furnace and the cold junctions should be at least 15 inches in all cases in which the heating of the cold junction is not automatically compensated. After inserting the couple the opening through the furnace wall should be closed by means of suitable luting-clay.

In certain instances, such as flues, it is necessary to use a long instrument in a horizontal position. A rail may then be placed across the flue, at a suitable place, to serve as a support and so to prevent drooping.

Liquid Element Thermocouples.—An investigation by the author and A. W. Grace has shown that the continuity of the E.M.F. produced by a rising temperature is not interrupted by fusion, except in the cases of bismuth and antimony, which both show an abrupt change in thermo-electric properties at the melting point. It would therefore appear feasible to measure temperatures by constructing a thermocouple so as to retain the circuit after fusion, the advantage gained being that the range is restricted by the boiling point of the metals instead of the melting point and higher readings are rendered possible. The boiling points of some of the common metals are appended:—

Metal.	Boiling Point.	
	Deg. C.	Deg. F
Aluminium	1800	3270
Silver	1955	3550
Tin	2270	4120
Copper	2310	4190
Nickel	2330	4225

Iron	2450	4440

From inspection of these figures, it will be seen that if a suitable couple could be obtained, common metals might be used to measure temperatures equalling or even exceeding the limit of the range covered by wire junctions of metals of the platinum series. Instead of using two metals, graphite might form one member of the couple, provided that no objection to its use existed on other grounds.

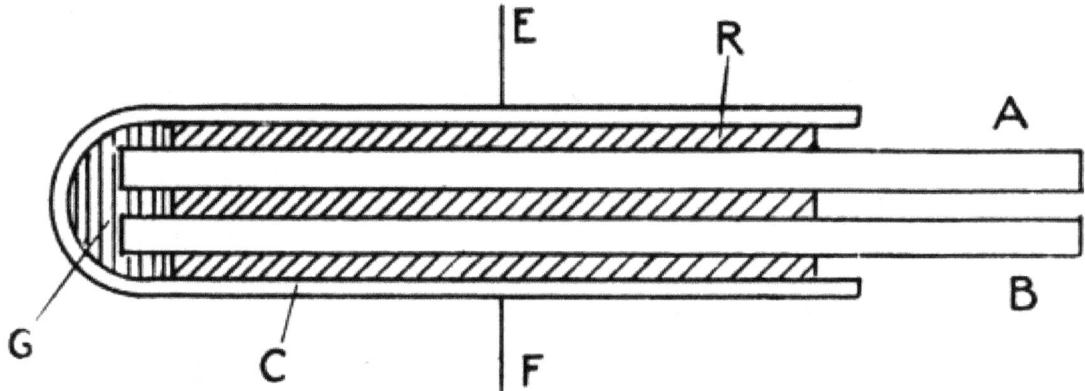

FIG. 9.—LIQUID-ELEMENT THERMOCOUPLE.

The form of thermocouple designed by the author to permit of the use of molten elements is shown in fig. 9. A rod of refractory material, R, is perforated longitudinally by two holes, down which are passed rods of the thermo-elements, A and B. The lower ends of A and B are inserted in a graphite block G, which is jointed on its upper face to R; the whole being surrounded by the refractory cover C. On either or both of the elements melting, the circuit is maintained through G, which serves also to prevent the mixing of A and B when molten, whilst not affecting the E.M.F. developed. In order to allow for the expansion of the metals on melting, A and B are made to fit loosely in R. When inserted in a furnace to a depth represented by EF, only the portion of the metals adjacent to the closed end will melt, the outer parts remaining solid. At present it has not been found possible to procure the refractory parts in a form suited to commercial use, but when this obstacle is overcome this type of thermocouple should prove of service for measuring temperatures beyond the scope of ordinary base-metal junctions.

Indicators for Thermo-electric Pyrometers.—As the electromotive force developed by a single junction when heated is small, a sensitive galvanometer is required to indicate the minute current flowing through the circuit. Delicate millivoltmeters, of the moving-coil type, are universally employed, as they possess the advantage of an evenly-divided scale combined with the requisite degree of sensitiveness. The original d'Arsonval galvanometer, consisting of a coil suspended by a metallic strip between the poles of a horse-shoe magnet, was used by Le Chatelier, who, by its aid, was enabled to lay the foundations of this branch of pyrometry. Three forms of this instrument are now in use, viz. (*a*) the suspended coil "mirror" type; (*b*) the suspended coil "pointer" type; and (*c*) the pivoted type. Examples of each will now be described.

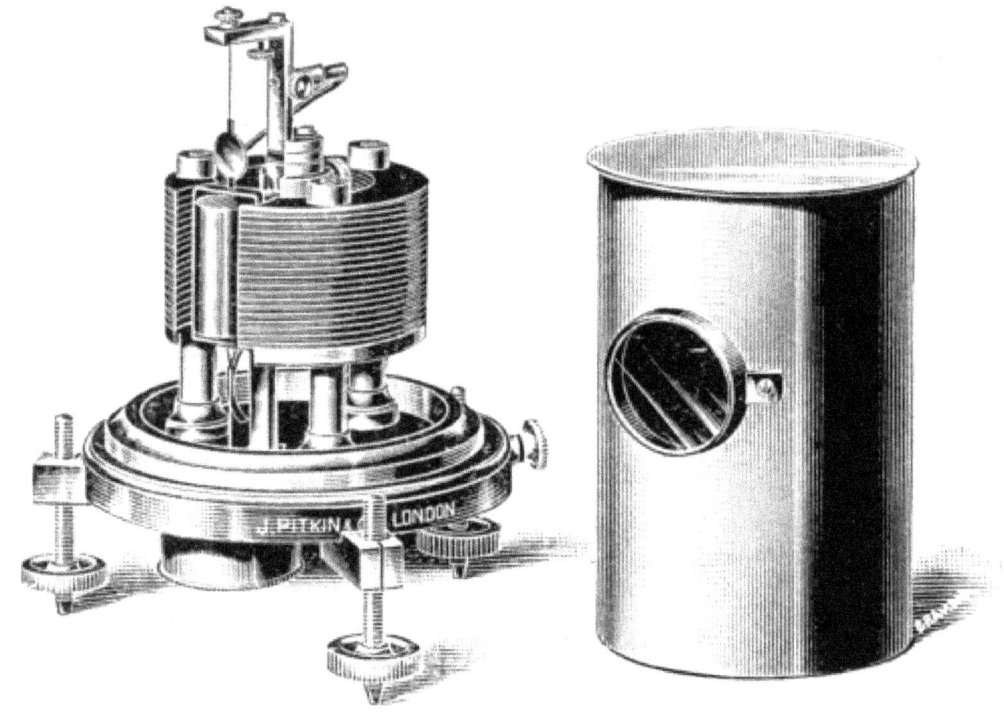

FIG. 10.—HOLDEN-D'ARSONVAL MIRROR GALVANOMETER.

Fig. 10 represents a mirror galvanometer working on the d'Arsonval principle, designed by Gen. Holden, F.R.S. The horse-shoe magnet is laminated, and an iron core, supported by a pillar, is placed between the poles. The coil, which moves in the space between the core and the poles of the magnet, is suspended by a thin, flat strip of phosphor-bronze, which carries a small circular mirror. A similar phosphor-bronze strip is fastened to the lower part of the coil, and is continued to an adjusting-screw in the base. The ends of the suspension strips communicate with the terminals of the galvanometer, and a current entering at one terminal passes through the metallic suspensions and the coil to the other. The effect of passing a current through the coil, which is located in a powerful magnetic field is to produce an axial movement tending to twist the suspension strips, which movement is greatly magnified by a spot of light reflected from the mirror on to a distant scale. When the current ceases, the untwisting of the strip restores the coil to its former position. Galvanometers of this type are remarkably "dead-beat" in action, that is, the movement and restoration of the coil are accomplished without vibration. A semi-transparent scale, placed at 1 metre distance, and 50 centimetres long, is suitable for use with this galvanometer. When used in workshops, it is necessary to protect a mirror galvanometer from the vibrations produced by machinery, which would cause the spot of light to become unsteady. The best method of effecting this is shown in fig. 11, which represents the mode of suspension devised by W. J. Lambert for use in the Royal Gun Factory, Woolwich Arsenal. The usual supports of the galvanometer are abolished, and the instrument suspended from the ring of a brass tripod, so as to keep three springs partly in compression. When suspended in this manner, a mirror galvanometer is quite suited to commercial use; in the quiet of the laboratory the ordinary supports may be employed. The advantage gained by using the mirror type is that a much longer scale is possible than with instruments furnished with a pointer, and hence greater accuracy in determining temperature readings may be secured.

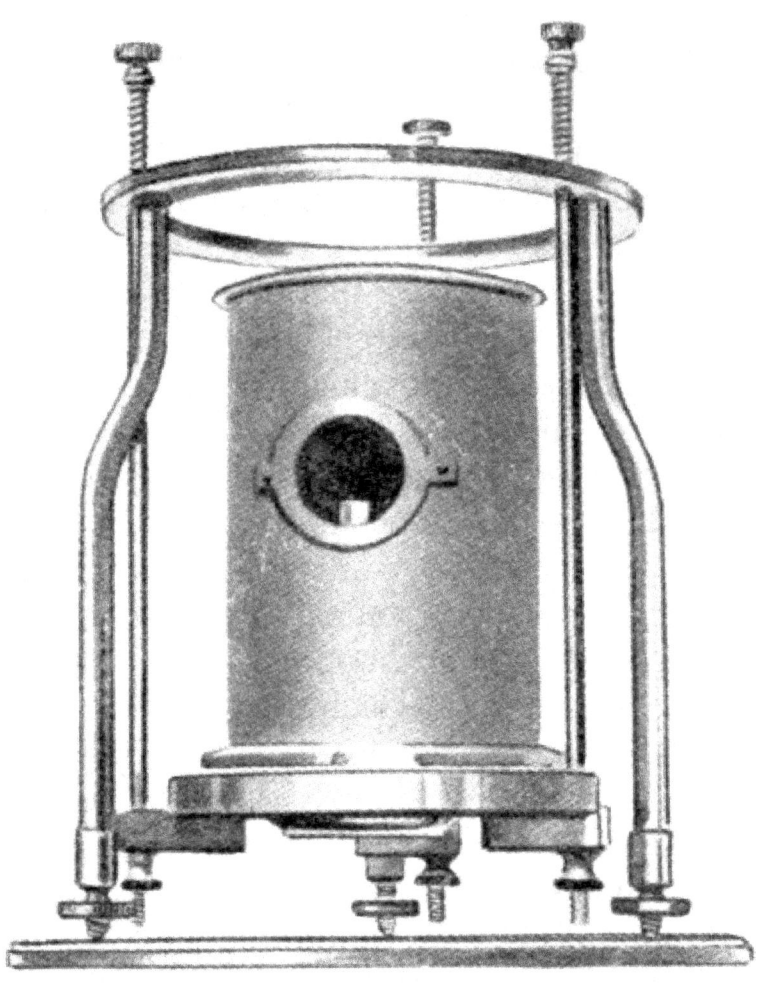

FIG. 11.—LAMBERT'S ANTI-VIBRATION STAND FOR GALVANOMETERS.

FIG. 12.—SIEMENS' THERMO-ELECTRIC INDICATOR.

In suspended coil instruments furnished with a pointer, the construction differs only in detail from the foregoing. In place of the mirror, a light pointer is attached to the suspension so as to rest on the coil and a scale is furnished over which the pointer moves. Fig. 12 is an example of this type, made by Messrs Siemens, the suspension being contained in the tube which rises from the body of the instrument. The maximum length of scale moved over by the extremity of the pointer is about 6 inches, as a longer and therefore heavier pointer would reduce the sensitiveness below the point requisite for thermo-electric work.

In the double-pivoted type, the suspension is eliminated, and pivots are fastened to each end of the moving coil which rest in bearings. The turning of the coil is made to compress a hair spring, made of phosphor-bronze; and when the current ceases the unwinding of this spring restores the coil to its former position. The coil carries a pointer which moves over a scale. These instruments are not so sensitive as those in which the coil is suspended, but can be made sufficiently sensitive to work with any kind of junction in practical use. The pivoted form is cheaper and stronger than the suspended type, and is used whenever sufficiently sensitive.

The "Uni-pivot" galvanometer, made by R. W. Paul, is shown in figs. 13 and 17. The coil, which carries the pointer, is circular, and moves round a spherical core of iron placed between the poles of the magnet. A hole is drilled in the iron core, and the coil rests on a single bearing at the bottom of this hole. A phosphor-bronze control-spring serves to restore the coil to the zero position. The lessened friction due to the use of a single pivot enables this instrument to be made very sensitive when needed, so that a relatively small rise in the temperature of a junction may cause the pointer to traverse the whole length of the scale.

FIG. 13.—PRINCIPLE OF UNI-PIVOT GALVANOMETER.

Special Features of Indicators.—All moving-coil instruments, whether suspended or pivoted, are liable to alteration of the zero point owing to what is termed "creep." The suspension strip, when first fixed in position, generally possesses a certain amount of initial torsion, which comes into operation gradually and causes a slight movement of the coil. Similarly, in a pivoted instrument, the strength or shape of the control-spring undergoes a gradual alteration at first, causing the pointer to move away from the zero position. For this reason adjusting arrangements are fitted by means of which the spot of light or pointer may be brought back to the zero. This creeping ceases after a time—often requiring twelve months—and if not subjected to any strain, error from this cause does not recur to any notable extent. With a mirror galvanometer it is better to move the scale, or turn the galvanometer round on its axis to restore the correct zero, rather than to twist the coil back; but with a fixed scale and pointer the only remedy is to turn the coil bodily round. In a single-pivot indicator constantly used in the author's laboratory, the creep amounted to a movement of the end of the pointer through an angle of 2 degrees in the first few months, since when, after the lapse of several years, no further alteration has occurred. It is advisable to test the zero point of an indicator from time to time by breaking the circuit, and if an error be discovered the pointer should be re-set, or an allowance made in taking a reading.

The resistance of an indicator should be so high that the readings should not be perceptibly altered by any fluctuations in the resistance of the circuit which may arise in practice. If leads of considerable length were used to connect the pyrometer with the indicator, and were subject to fairly large alterations of temperature, the consequent changes in the resistance of such leads would be noticeable on a low-resistance indicator; and similarly, if a pyrometer were inserted at different depths in a furnace at separate times, thus heating up varying lengths of the junction wires, a discrepancy would arise for the same reason. The resistance of an indicator, however, cannot be raised beyond a certain point without reducing the sensitiveness below the required limit. A mirror galvanometer of the type described may have a resistance—partly in the coil and partly in an added series resistance—of 1000 ohms or more, and still be sufficiently sensitive; and in the latest types of instruments provided with pointers the resistance may be made as high as 1000 ohms, although it is more usually 400 to 500 ohms. Many indicators are in use, however, in which the resistance is 100 ohms or less. As, from Ohm's law, the current varies inversely as the total resistance in the circuit, any alteration in resistance should be small relatively to the total to render the error negligible. This point is made clear in the following example:—

Example.—A thermocouple and leads have a resistance of 5 ohms and are subject to alterations amounting to 1 ohm. To find the errors resulting when indicators of resistances 800, 400, and 50 ohms respectively are used.

From Ohm's law, C = E/R, the variation in C, with E constant, will be 1 in 805, 1 in 405, and 1 in 55 respectively. As the indications are proportional to the current, the alterations caused will be approximately ⅛ per cent., ¼ per cent., and 2 per cent. The first two may be ignored; the last may be quite serious and lead to the failure of an operation.

It will be seen from the foregoing that low-resistance indicators should only be used for fixed thermocouples and short leads not subject to temperature changes, or, in other words, in a circuit of fixed resistance.

The resistance of an indicator, when unknown, may be found by the following method, suggested by the author:—A resistance box is joined at one end to one terminal of the indicator. To the other terminal a fairly stout iron wire, 18 inches long, is connected, and a similar length of constantan wire is coupled to the other end of the resistance box. The free ends of the wires are twisted into a junction which is dipped into boiling water. The deflection obtained with no resistance in the box (D_1) is noted, and resistances (R) are then unplugged until the deflection (D_2) is approximately one-half of D_1. The resistance (G) of the indicator, ignoring that of the wires, is then given by the formula

$$G = \frac{D_2 R}{D_1 - D_2}$$

as may readily be proved from Ohm's law, E being constant. This method is extremely simple and reasonably accurate.

Reliable indicators are now procurable from many instrument-makers at a comparatively small cost, progress in this direction having been most marked in recent years, particularly in the case of pivoted instruments. The most convenient form for workshop use is made with an edgewise scale (fig. 14) and may be placed in a suitable position fixed to a bracket. The flat-scale pattern is preferable for use on a laboratory table, or for a portable pyrometer. The sector pattern is also good for workshop use, the dial being visible from a distance.

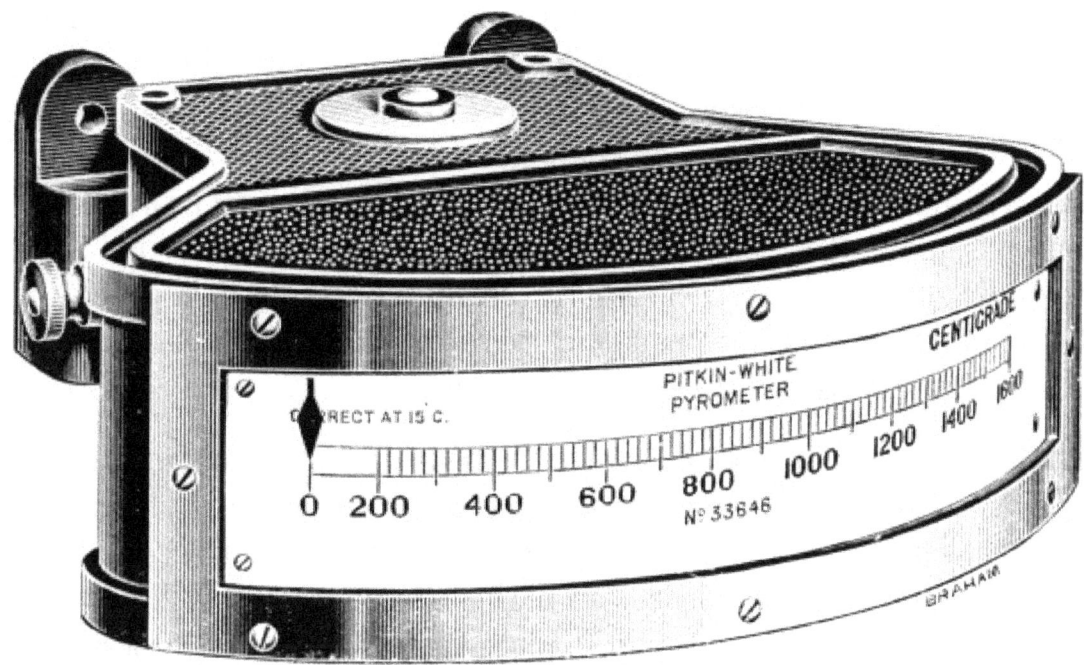

FIG. 14.—INDICATOR WITH EDGEWISE SCALE

Standardizing of Indicators to read Temperatures directly. —The temperature scale of an indicator, for use with a given thermal couple, is always marked by the maker in the case of instruments furnished with a pointer, and, generally speaking, is correct within reasonable limits. It is customary and necessary to send with the instrument a statement of the cold-junction temperature for which the markings are correct; say 20° C. or 60° F. The user should then endeavour to maintain the cold junction at this specified temperature when taking a reading, or otherwise a considerable error may be introduced. It is highly desirable, however, that the user should be able to perform the standardizing himself, if only for checking purposes; and when using a mirror galvanometer as indicator it is necessary to standardize on the spot at which the instrument is fixed. Ability to prepare a temperature scale is further useful, inasmuch as any good millivoltmeter, of range 0 to 20 millivolts, may be used for thermo-electric work of all kinds, and may be calibrated for different junctions, a suitable series resistance being added to enable E.M.F.'s higher than 20 millivolts to be measured. Such an instrument may thus be made extremely useful, both in the workshop and laboratory.

Standardization may be effected either by subjecting the hot junction to several known temperatures, and noticing the deflections corresponding thereto; or by measuring the electromotive force developed by the junction, and calculating the corresponding temperature from a formula which is known to hold for the range comprehended by the instrument. The former method is simpler; and if carefully conducted is quite accurate. The latter method possesses the advantage that readings in millivolts may be translated directly into temperatures when the constants of a given thermal couple are known. It is now usual to mark indicators with a double scale, one reading millivolts and the other temperatures.

Standardization by Fixed Points.—Taking any millivoltmeter which, with a maximum of 20 millivolts at the terminals, will give a full scale deflection, the first step is to arrange that the pointer (or spot of light) shall just remain on the scale at the highest temperature to be attained by the junction. This may be done by placing the hot junction in boiling water and noting the deflection obtained, either in millivolts or equal arbitrary divisions, and also the temperature of the cold junction. The deflection observed is due to a difference of temperature ($100-t$) deg. C, where t is the temperature of the cold junction. If the highest temperature to be measured is 10 times ($100-t$), the deflection should be rather less than $\frac{1}{10}$ of the scale, and similarly for any other required temperature limit. If the observed deflection exceed this proportion, a series resistance should be added until the correct value is obtained. This resistance is then permanently installed in the circuit for use with the junction under trial.

Before proceeding further it is necessary to consider whether the pyrometer is to possess a single cold junction of ascertainable temperature (as in fig. 6), or whether it will be arranged with two cold junctions in the head, as in fig. 4. In the former case it is simpler to prepare a "difference" scale; that is, one which reads differences of temperature between the hot and cold junctions, from which the temperature of the hot end may be obtained by adding to the difference that of the cold junction. In the latter case the cold end should be kept by artificial means at the temperature likely to be attained in practice—say 25° C.—a water-bath being suitable for this purpose. It is advisable to remove the shield of the pyrometer when standardizing, so as to expose the hot junction, as closer readings can then be taken.

A number of materials—preferably cheap—of known boiling points or melting points are then selected from a table of fixed points (page 16) so as to give about six points, distributed fairly evenly over the scale. As an example, if it were desired to prepare a temperature scale from 0° to 1000° C., the following might be chosen:—

Substance and Condition.	Temperature.	
Water at boiling point	100° C.	212° F.
Tin at melting point	232	449
Zinc at melting point	419	786
Antimony at melting point	631	1167
Common salt at melting point	800	1472
Copper at melting point (covered with graphite)	1084	1983

The hot junction is allowed to attain these temperatures successively, and the corresponding deflection in each case is noted. It is then possible to divide up the whole of the scale to read temperatures directly.

The first reading is taken by placing the junction in a vessel of boiling water, and for a locality near sea level it is not necessary in ordinary work to take account of fluctuations in the boiling point due to alterations of atmospheric pressure. To ensure that the other readings are taken when the substances are exactly at the melting point, the procedure is as follows: about 2-3 lb. of the substance are melted in a salamander crucible, and a small fireclay tube, closed at one end, is inserted in the molten mass. The hot junction is placed in the fireclay tube, and the intervening space filled with asbestos fibre. Great care must be taken not to let the junction touch the fused substance. The crucible is now allowed to cool, and a reading of the deflection taken every half-minute. When the substance is exactly at its solidifying point—identical in general with the melting point—the deflection remains stationary for several consecutive readings, owing to the liberation of latent heat of fusion in sufficient quantity to balance the loss by radiation. This stationary reading is noted for each substance, and represents the deflection given when the hot junction is at the temperature corresponding to the melting point, and the cold junction or junctions at the temperature existing when the observation is made. For melting the materials, a Davies furnace with a large Teclu or Meker burner is convenient up to 850° C.; but to melt the copper a blast lamp is requisite. The molten mass may be allowed to cool in the furnace.

From these observations a calibration curve may be drawn either for differences between hot and cold junctions, or for a steady temperature of the cold junctions. Two sets of data are appended to illustrate the procedure.

Temperature of Hot Junction.	Pyrometer 1. Iron-constantan. (Series resistance in galvanometer circuit.)			Pyrometer 2. Platinum-iridioplatinum.	
	Deflection.	Cold Junction.	Difference.	Deflection.	Cold Junction.
100° C.	8·9	15° C.	85° C.	5·5	Constant at 25° C.
232	21·8	17	215	15·6	
419	40·6	19	400	29·4	
631	63·8	19	612	45·5	
800	83·0	20	780	59·0	
1084	...	...	...	82·0	

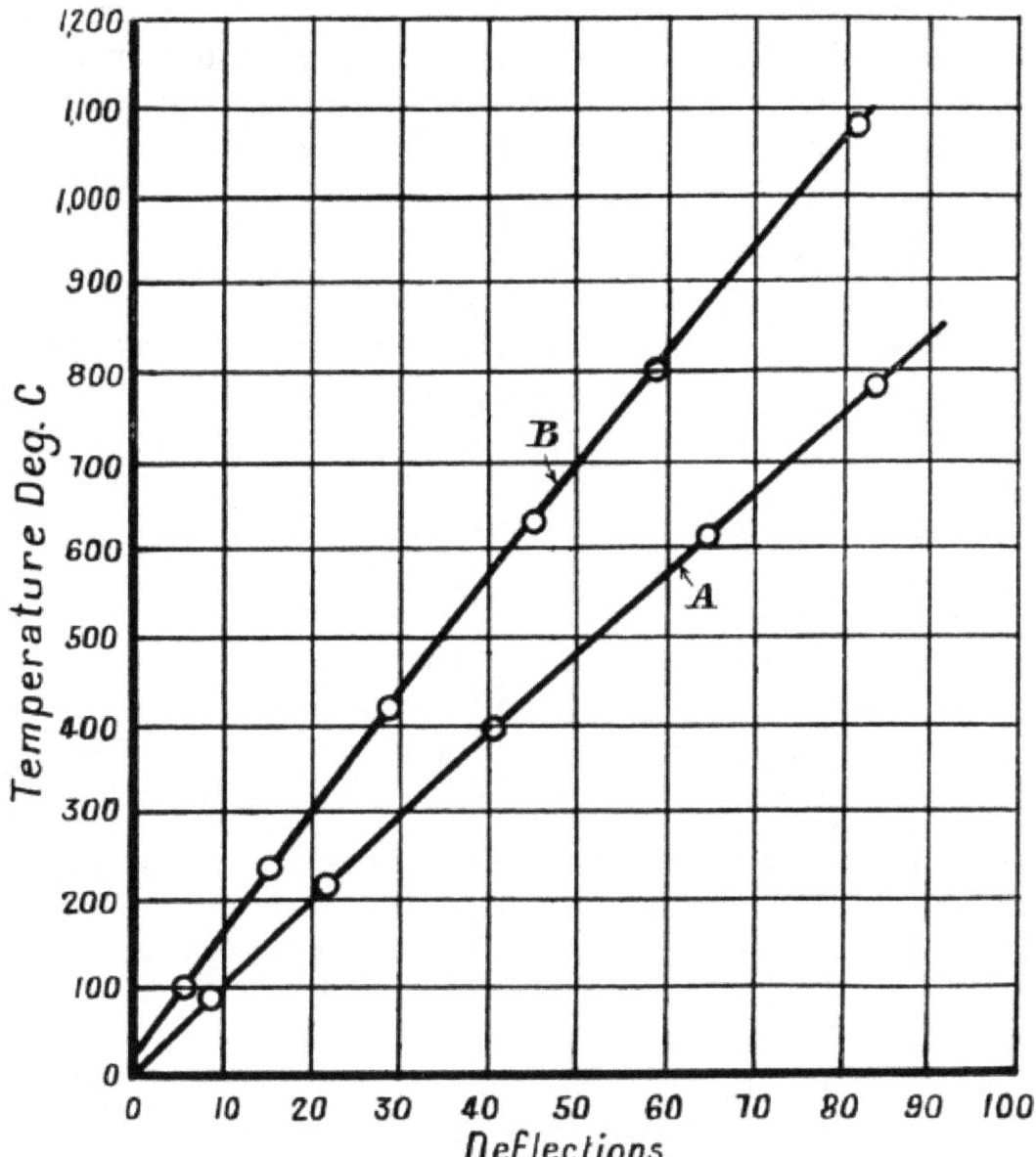

FIG. 15.—CALIBRATION CURVES FOR TWO THERMO-ELECTRIC PYROMETERS.

Fig. 15, A, is a calibration curve for thermocouple 1, connecting deflections with corresponding differences between the temperatures of the hot and cold junctions. In order to read from this curve the temperature of the hot end, the reading corresponding to the observed deflection is added to the existing temperature of the cold junction. Thus if a deflection of 56 divisions were obtained with the cold junction at 25°, the temperature of the hot junction would be (540 + 25) = 565° C. The advantage of this method of calibration is that it is unnecessary to take precautions to keep the cold junction at a steady temperature; and when a single cold junction is used, as in fig. 6, this plan should always be followed. It will be noted that this curve passes through zero, as no deflection represents no difference of temperature.

Fig. 15, B, represents the calibration curve for pyrometer 2, and is such that direct readings may be obtained corresponding to any given deflection, for a cold junction temperature of 25°. This curve, therefore, cuts the axis of zero deflection at 25°, as no deflection corresponds to the condition when both hot and cold junctions are at 25°. This method of calibration may be used with advantage for couples of the type shown in fig. 4, where two cold junctions exist in the head, and the simple rule of adding the cold junction temperature does not apply. Many suggestions have been made for correcting for alterations in the temperature of the cold end of such a couple, but none are accurate, and it is necessary to keep this part at the temperature of standardization to secure correct readings. In both of the above calibrations the galvanometer used possessed a scale divided into 100 equal arbitrary divisions.

In making permanent temperature scales from these curves to attach to the existing galvanometer scale, intervals of 100° may be taken and marked opposite to the corresponding divisions on the existing scale. Each 100° may then be equally subdivided into as many parts as the length of scale permits, and numbered at suitable intervals. If the junction used yield a calibration curve departing greatly from a straight line, every 50° interval should be taken, or, if necessary, every 25°. In the examples given both curves are nearly straight lines in the working region, viz. 400° to 800° for the iron-constantan junction, and 500° to 1100° for the platinum-iridioplatinum.

One precaution necessary in standardizing an indicator by this method is to ensure that the metals used are pure, as impurities lower the melting points. If ordered as "pure" from any dealer of repute, the metals will generally be found satisfactory. The common salt used should be the ordinary salt sold in blocks, and not a prepared table salt. A second precaution, when observing melting points, is to guard against a possible error due to the substance becoming "surfused" or "overcooled"; in which case the temperature falls below the ordinary freezing point before solidification commences. When freezing occurs, however, the temperature rises to and remains at the true melting point, and an increase of deflection following a gradual fall always indicates overcooling. The higher deflection then attained is the true freezing point. Antimony frequently overcools to 600° before freezing, but on setting rises to the correct figure—631°. All metals and salts are liable to overcooling occasionally.

Standardization by Measurement of E.M.F.—It has been found, as the result of experiments, that the relation between the E.M.F. developed by a junction and its temperature—under constant conditions of the cold junction—may be expressed approximately by a formula as under:—

$$\log E = A \log t + B \quad \text{(Holman's formula)},$$

where E = electromotive force in microvolts, t = temperature in Centigrade degrees, and A and B are constants depending upon the junction. With certain junctions this formula may be applied over the working part of the scale with an error not exceeding 2° C., but with others the discrepancy is greater. In order to determine the constants A and B, it is necessary to measure the E.M.F. at two known temperatures, which should be chosen as far apart as possible in the working region. When these constants are known, a measurement of E enables the temperature t to be found by calculation.

Example.—Le Chatelier found that a junction at the temperature of melted aluminium (657° C.) gave 6200 microvolts; at the melting point of copper in air (1062° C.) the figure was 10580. Applying in the above formula

$$\log 6200 = A \log 657 + B$$

and

$$\log 10580 = A \log 1062 + B,$$

the value of A is 1·2196 and of B 0·302, as may be found by taking logarithms and solving for A and B.

The values of the constants A and B vary for different junctions, and also for different melts of what are reputed to be the same materials. When once determined for a quantity of homogeneous wires, to which the formula applies with sufficient accuracy, it is evident that an indicator with a millivolt scale may be made to read temperatures directly without any necessity for further experiment, although it is always advisable to take one check reading at a fixed point in the working range.

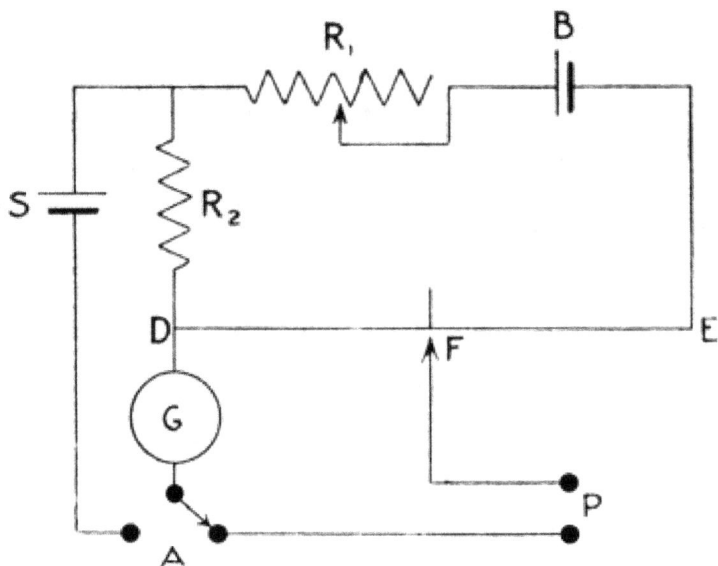

FIG. 16.—POTENTIOMETER METHOD OF MEASURING E. M. F.

In order to determine the E.M.F. of a junction at different temperatures, the potentiometer method is used, in which the E.M.F. of the test-couple is balanced against the known E.M.F. furnished by a constant cell. The circuit is shown in fig. 16, in which B is an accumulator which sends a current through the resistances R_1, R_2, and the calibrated wire DE. The cold ends of the couple are attached at P so as to be in opposition to B, and in this branch of the circuit are included a sensitive galvanometer G and a portion of the wire DE. A standard cadmium cell, S, is connected between R_1 and R_2 at one end, and may be put in circuit with the galvanometer through the switch A. In commencing, S is connected to the galvanometer and R_1 adjusted until no deflection is obtained on G. The switch A is now moved over to the circuit of the couple, and the terminal F moved along the wire until zero deflection is again obtained. The E.M.F. of the couple is determined from the relation

$$\frac{\text{E of junction}}{} = \frac{\text{Resistance of DF}}{}$$

By exposing the hot end of the junction to successive standard temperatures, and maintaining the cold ends at a known constant temperature, the necessary data for inclusion in a formula may be obtained.

In fixing a permanent temperature scale, calculated from the formula, to a millivoltmeter, it must be remembered that the values given by the experiment are absolute, and independent of the resistance of the circuit composed of the thermo-element and galvanometer. On the other hand, a millivoltmeter is marked to read difference of potential at its terminals; and if in series with a junction and leads of notable resistance, its indications will not be the E.M.F. of the junction. An example will make this point clear.

Example.—A millivoltmeter has a resistance of 100 ohms, and is marked to read P.D. at its terminals. A thermocouple and leads connected to the millivoltmeter have a resistance of 5 ohms. To find the relation between the true E.M.F. of the junction and the readings of the indicator.

If E = the E.M.F. developed by the junction, and V, the reading of the millivoltmeter, = P.D. at its terminals, then the current in the circuit = $E/105$ = $V/100$; and $V = (100/105)E$. That is, the readings are lower by 5 per cent. than the true E.M.F. of the junction. In the same way a low resistance voltmeter, if applied to a cell of high resistance, shows a lower reading than the E.M.F. of the cell.

This example indicates how a table connecting true E.M.F.'s with reading in millivolts may be calculated when the resistances concerned are known. It is presumed, in preparing a scale in this manner, that the resistance of the couple will not be subject to such alterations as to affect the reading.

The advantages of this method of calibration are manifest when a number of junctions are being made from a given batch of wires, as it is only necessary to divide the scale of the indicator so as to represent millivolts—a simple operation—and then to attach a temperature scale. This procedure is much more expeditious than standardizing each indicator at several fixed points when a number are concerned, but for a single junction the fixed point method is easier. The potentiometer method of measuring E.M.F. may also be used to determine temperatures in place of an indicator, and is of great service in cases where very accurate readings are specially required, being far more delicate in detecting small differences of temperature than an indicator. Special potentiometers for thermo-electric work are made by the Cambridge and Paul Instrument Company, Siemens, and others, and are useful in conducting accurate research, but are too elaborate for workshop or ordinary laboratory practice.

Cold Junction Compensators.—The necessity for paying attention to the cold junction has led to various attempts to compensate automatically for changes of temperature at this part of the pyrometer. A thermometer located near the cold junction, as in fig. 6, is all that is needed to correct a two-junction circuit; but when a three-junction circuit is used a correct reading is not secured by adding the excess temperature of the thermometer over the calibration temperature to the reading on the indicator. In Bristol's arrangement a mercury thermometer, with a large bulb and wide stem, is stationed at the cold junction, and participates in any temperature change. In the stem is placed a loop of thin platinum wire, which forms part of the pyrometer circuit. When the mercury is heated it expands up the stem and short-circuits a portion of the loop, thereby diminishing the resistance of the pyrometer circuit, and tending to increase the deflection on the indicator. Simultaneously the cold junction will be heated, tending to diminish the current, and so to cause a less deflection. By adjustment these two tendencies may be counterbalanced, so that the reading is unaffected, but such adjustment will only apply to a given E.M.F., and therefore to one temperature of the hot junction. Hence this method fails in general application.

Peake's compensated leads are intended to remedy cold-junction errors by transferring this junction, in effect, to the galvanometer. They are used for pyrometers in which the platinum metals are employed, and consist of wires of two different alloys of copper and nickel, which connect the cold end to the indicator. These alloys are such that the electromotive forces set up at the junctions in the head—Pt and Cu-Ni 1, and Pt-Ir with Cu-Ni 2—are equal and opposite at all working temperatures, and hence changes at the cold junctions do not affect the reading. At the indicator, however, temperature changes would cause an alteration in deflection; but as the indicator is generally placed well away from the furnace, and is not liable to notable heating or cooling, the possible errors are greatly reduced by the use of these leads. They are obviously of no value for use with base-metal pyrometers, as the wires used in such may be prolonged to the indicator, with an identical result.

FIG. 17.—DARLING'S COMPENSATOR, FITTED TO GALVANOMETER.

An automatic compensator for use with base-metal pyrometers has been devised by the author, and is illustrated in figs. 17 and 18. A spiral made of a compound strip of two metals is attached to the needle of the indicator, and coils or uncoils when cooled or heated, thereby moving the pointer over the scale. The length of the spiral is such that an alteration of a given number of degrees in its temperature moves the pointer by the same number of degrees on the scale—or, in other words, the temperature scale of the pyrometer is identical with that of the spiral. The metals forming the junction are continued, in the form of wires, to the interior of the galvanometer, where a cold junction is formed, which will always possess the same temperature as the spiral. The scale is constructed to represent differences of temperature between the hot and cold junctions, and before coupling up the pyrometer the pointer indicates the temperature of the spiral; that is, of the cold junction. On connecting the thermocouple the pointer is moved by the coil of the indicator through an amount represented by the difference in temperature between the two junctions, and therefore finally indicates the temperature of the hot junction.

FIG. 18.—INDICATOR FITTED WITH DARLING'S COMPENSATOR.

Example.—If the cold junction were at 20°, the pointer, before connecting the couple, would indicate 20° on the scale. If the hot junction were 580° hotter than the cold, then on completing the circuit the pointer would move 580 additional degrees along the scale, so that the figure indicated would be (20 + 580) = 600°, the temperature of the hot junction. If now the indicator were heated by 10°, the spiral would tend to augment the deflection by 10°, but simultaneously the deflection due to the junctions would fall off by 10°, and the reading would still be 600°.

This method of compensation renders the readings independent of the cold junction, and, in addition to its use for high temperatures, enables ordinary and low temperatures to be read simply and correctly, as will be shown later. The spiral is located in the tower rising from the top of the indicator in fig. 18.

In Paul's method of compensation the thermocouple and indicator are placed across a Wheatstone bridge, two arms of which contain resistances of copper, whilst the resistances in the other two arms are of manganin. Any change in temperature at the cold junction is shared by these four resistances, and, whilst affecting the resistance of the copper parts, no change is caused in the manganin parts, as this alloy has a negligible temperature coefficient. If, therefore, the bridge were initially balanced at 20° C., and the temperature rose to 30°, the increased resistance of the copper would destroy the balance, and permit of a small current passing through the indicator. A fall to 10°, by diminishing the resistance of the copper, would cause an equal current to pass through the indicator in the opposite direction. The amount of this current is arranged so as to add the rise in temperature of the cold junction to the reading of the indicator in the one case, and to subtract the fall in the other, thus retaining true readings for the cold-junction temperature at which the couple was standardized.

Constant Temperature Cold Junctions.—If the cold junction can be kept at a steady temperature, compensators are unnecessary, but no good practical means of achieving this end has yet been devised. Water-cooled heads have already been referred to; but in many situations the connecting-pipes entailed would be objectionable, and hence this arrangement is not greatly used. An alternative method, suggested by Prof. A. Zeleny, is to bury the cold junction in the ground. Recent experiments, conducted at Cambridge by R. S. Whipple, showed that a junction buried 10 feet deep did not vary in temperature by more than 2° C. over a period of three years. This has led to the adoption of buried junctions in special cases; but it is probable that much greater variations would be experienced in the ground beneath large furnaces, in which case the advantages of this procedure would be lost. A common workshop method is to locate the cold junction in a thermos flask filled with oil, when a temperature constant to 2° C. may be secured, although the changes in the temperature of the surrounding atmosphere may be as great as 150 C. For special work, ice may be used in the thermos flask, thus securing absolute constancy; but this procedure is not feasible in ordinary works practice.

Special-Range Indicators.—When the working range of a pyrometer is from 600° C. upwards, it is evident that the part of the scale occupied by the first 600° is useless, and that it would be an advantage if the whole scale could be utilised for the special working range, so as to secure more exact readings. This may be accomplished by a "set-up" against the movement of the pointer caused by the thermocouple, so as to prevent any motion over the scale until an assigned temperature is reached. For example, a junction developing 12 millivolts at 1000° C. may be coupled to an indicator in which the full-scale deflection of the pointer is produced by 6 millivolts. If an E.M.F. of 6 millivolts be opposed to the junction, no deflection will occur until the temperature at which the couple develops 6 millivolts is reached—when the opposing E.M.F. will be overcome. This temperature may be 500° C., so that the whole scale may be divided up between 500° and 1000°. The length of the indicator scale is thus effectively doubled; and by using different values for the set-up, it is evident that any desired range may be obtained within the limits of sensitivity of the indicator. The method of procuring the opposing E.M.F. varies with different makers. The Cambridge and Paul Instrument Company employ a dry cell and a series resistance, connected so as to oppose the thermocouple; and by adjusting the resistance any desired set-up may be obtained, the value of which, in degrees, may be read off by connecting the cell and resistance to the indicator, the couple having been switched out of the circuit. Thus, to adjust for a range of 500°-1000° on an indicator giving full-scale deflection for 500°, the resistance is regulated so that the cell alone causes the pointer to move to the end of the scale. The method adopted by Paul consists of suitable resistances inserted in a Wheatstone bridge, which may be thrown off the balance, and thus cause an opposing E.M.F. of the correct amount at the terminals of the indicator.

A mechanical set-up has been introduced by the Cambridge and Paul Instrument Company, the indicator in this case having a suspended coil. By turning a milled-head a twist may be given to the suspending strip, and by the turning of a second head the pointer may be brought back to zero, retaining the initial twist, which is opposed to that produced by the current due to the couple. Thus, if the imposed twist were such as to move the pointer to the 400° mark on the scale, the temperature indicated by the junction would be the observed reading plus 400. By this method it is possible to obtain any desired range within the limits of the indicator. The danger of producing errors due to "creeping" is said to be negligible.

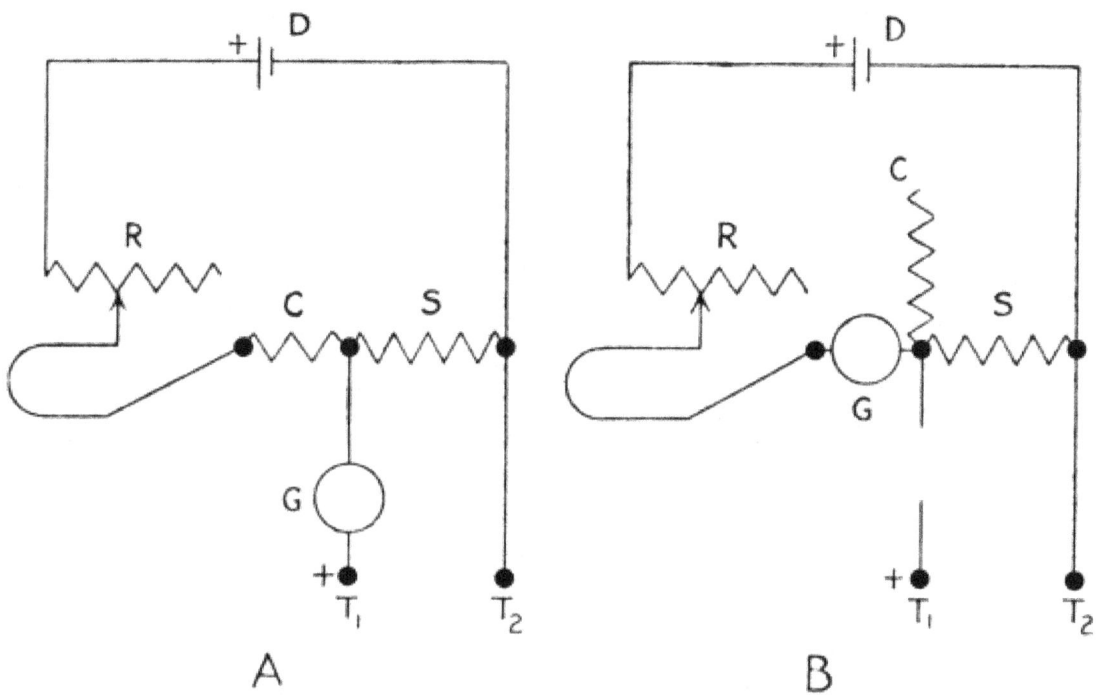

FIG. 19.—CIRCUIT OF NORTHRUP'S "PYROVOLTER."

Potentiometer Indicators.—The advantage of measuring E.M.F. by the potentiometer method is that the result is independent of the resistance of the circuit under test, whereas an indicator is affected by changes in the resistance of the circuit in which it is inserted. When long leads are used to connect a couple to its indicator, notable errors may be caused by the varying resistance of the leads, due to changing temperature; and, in addition, the resistance of the couple-wires varies according to temperature and depth of insertion in the furnace. Attempts have therefore been made to produce indicators based on the potentiometer principle, suitable for workshop use, and one form, known as Northrup's "Pyrovolter," is arranged as shown in fig. 19, A. A cell D sends a current through a rheostat R, a copper coil C, and a manganin coil S. The copper coil has the same resistance as the copper winding of the indicator G. The couple is connected, with G in circuit, across the manganin coil S, the resistance of this material being unaffected by temperature. By adjusting R until no deflection is shown on G, the drop of volts across S is made equal to the E.M.F. of the couple. To measure this drop, a key is pressed, altering the circuit as shown in B, the indicator being now in series with S and the couple detached. The value of the current passing through S is unchanged, as the indicator coil has the same resistance as the copper coil C, which it now replaces. The deflection on G indicates the value of this current, and, as the drop of volts across S is proportional to the current, G may be marked off to read E.M.F. and the corresponding temperature of the junction. The advantages claimed are that the indicator may be used with any type of junction, and is unaffected by temperature changes in the circuit. A similar instrument is made by the Brown Company of Philadelphia. Up to the present potentiometer indicators have not been adopted to any extent in Britain, and the adjustments necessary to obtain a reading must be accounted a distinct drawback from a workshop standpoint.

Recorders for Thermo-electric Pyrometers.—It is frequently of importance to know not only the existing temperature of a furnace, but also the fluctuations to which it is subject. Continuous observation of a pyrometer would involve too much labour, and it is therefore evident that an automatic recorder would possess many advantages in such cases. A continuous record shows whether the attendant has maintained the temperature between the prescribed limits, and furnishes a permanent history of a given operation, which often serves as a guide to future procedure.

The first successful recorder, suggested by Sir W. Roberts-Austen and designed by Gen. Holden, F.R.S., was used in conjunction with a mirror galvanometer. In its original form, the spot of light from the mirror was made to fall on a sensitized plate, to which a gradual vertical motion was conveyed by connecting the dark slide to a water-float by means of a chain and pulley. The float was placed in a tank of water, which was gradually emptied through a tap, causing the float to sink and the plate to rise. If the deflection of the spot of light remained steady, a vertical straight line was traced on the plate, fluctuations producing a sinuous line. Trials at known temperatures enabled a standard plate to be obtained, divided into degrees, which could be superposed on a trial plate, and the temperatures thus determined. Much valuable work was accomplished with this recorder by Roberts-Austen for the Alloys Research Committee of the Institution of Mechanical Engineers.

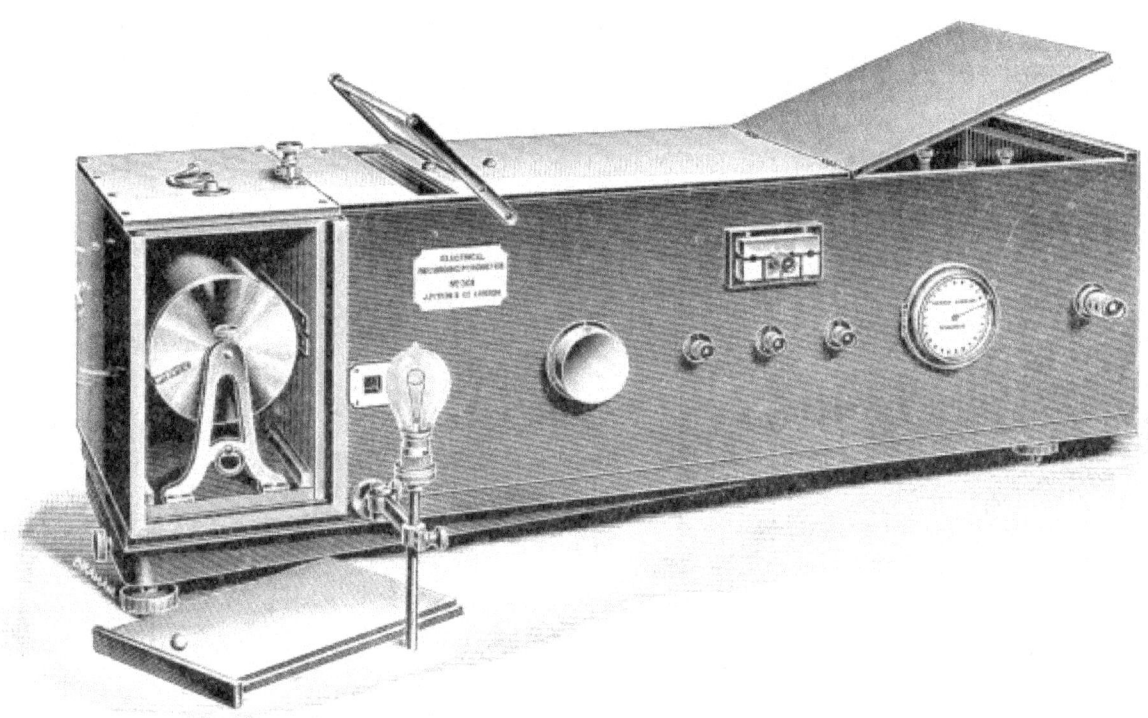

FIG. 20.—ROBERTS-AUSTEN RECORDER.

In its modern form (fig. 20) the photographic plate is replaced by a sheet of sensitized paper wound round a drum which rotates at a known rate —say, once in 12 hours—by means of internal clockwork, shown to the left of the figure. The galvanometer is placed at the opposite end, and the mirror is illuminated by means of an electric lamp placed externally, the rays from which are reflected from a prism in the interior on to the mirror. The ray of light leaving the mirror is broken into two portions, one of which passes through a narrow slit on to the sensitized paper, whilst the other portion is reflected on to a ground-glass scale on the lid, divided so as to read temperatures. In this manner the arrangement serves not only as a recorder, but also indicates the existing temperature without necessitating the examination of the sensitized paper. The whole arrangement is made impervious to light, so that it may be used in daylight. A dark room is necessary for fixing the records. When desired, records of two or more pyrometers may be taken on the same sheet, a clockwork device being used to switch each instrument in turn on to the galvanometer for a given period, an external dial indicating which pyrometer is for the time being in circuit.

Whilst it is a drawback to the use of this recorder that the record is not visible, the use of a mirror galvanometer confers a high degree of sensitiveness to the instrument, not possessed by the recorders to be described subsequently.

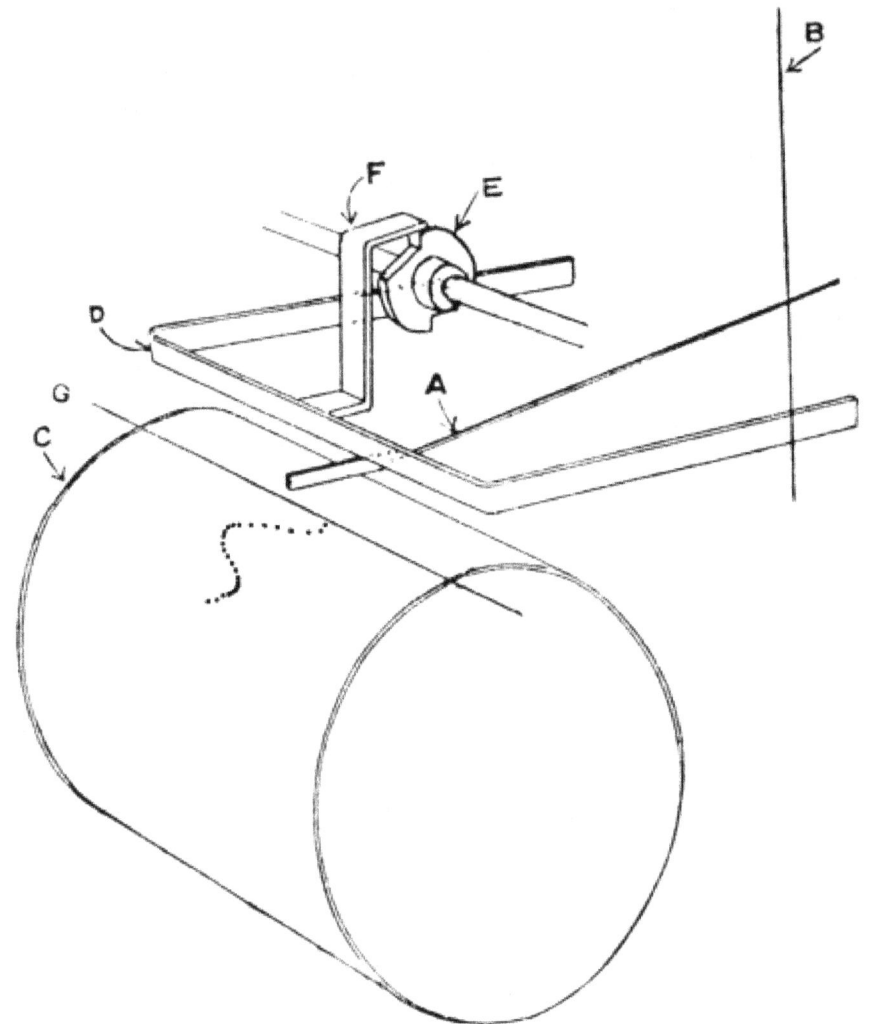

FIG. 21.—PRINCIPLE OF THREAD RECORDER.

The Thread Recorder.—In this instrument an intermittent record is secured in ink, possessing the advantages of visibility during the period over which readings are taken, and of permanence without subsequent treatment of the chart. The principle is shown in fig. 21, where A is a boom terminating in a V-shaped piece of ivory, and attached to the galvanometer suspension B. By means of a cam E, rotated by clockwork, a bar D is made to descend at stated intervals, pressing the end of A on to an inked thread G, and causing the thread to touch a paper wound round the drum C. This drum rotates on its axis once in 25 hours by the action of internal clockwork. The continued rotation of the cam E alternately raises and depresses the boom A, leaving it free for a sufficient time to enable it to attain the position it would occupy if the mechanism were absent. The thread G is passed over pulleys, and is wound round through an ink-well, so that the portion opposite A is always moist. With the bar D descending every two minutes, the successive dots form a nearly continuous line. The paper on C is divided horizontally into temperatures, and vertically into time units, so that the temperature existing at any given time may readily be ascertained. The front of the bar D, or a separate strip parallel to it, is divided so as to enable temperatures to be read without reference to the chart. The actual instrument is shown in fig. 22. When several simultaneous records are required, the drum C is extended, and other galvanometers introduced, to which the separate pyrometers are connected. Several records can be taken on one chart by introducing a clockwork mechanism to couple each pyrometer in turn to the one galvanometer.

Fig. 22.—Thread Recorder.

Fig. 23.—Siemens' Recorder.

The Siemens Recorder.—In this instrument (fig. 23) the boom from the galvanometer terminates in a knife-edge, and moves over a thin horizontal rail, the top of which is rounded. Between the rail and the boom are placed an inking ribbon and a paper chart, which is moved forward by clockwork. A chopper-bar, also actuated by clockwork, descends at about half-minute intervals, and depresses the end of the galvanometer boom, thus producing a small dot on the chart. The paper is 12 cms. wide and 40 yards long; it is divided into time and temperature units, and moves forward at the rate of 2 cms. per hour. Levelling screws are fixed to the base of the recorder.

FIG. 24.—FOSTER'S RECORDER.

Foster's Recorder.—Foster's recorder (fig. 24) is designed for use with base-metal couples of the nickel-chromium type, known as Hoskin's alloys, which yield an E.M.F. about five times as large as a platinum-rhodioplatinum couple. The force available in this case enables the coil of the galvanometer to be pivoted in a horizontal position, the pointer being vertical, and yet to be sufficiently sensitive. The chart is mounted on a vertical plate which rotates on its axis, the time ordinates taking the form of concentric circles, which are cut at an angle by the temperature ordinates. At the terminus of the pointer is placed a small capillary tube, fitted with an inked wick, which, when pressed upon the chart, makes a mark. The presser-bar is curved to the same radius as the pointer, and carries a pad wetted with ink, so that at each depression the supply of ink to the wick is replenished by an amount equal to that imparted to the chart. This recorder is sometimes fitted with special contacts, so that when the correct temperature exists an electric lamp with a white bulb remains lighted; whereas when too low or too high a green or red lamp is lit up, and an alarm thus given. Such an addition involves the use of a relay circuit, but is advisable in cases where expensive articles might suffer if overheated. It can be modified to permit of several simultaneous records being taken, and possesses the advantage that the whole chart is visible at any time. On the other hand, the circular coordinates may be accounted a drawback by some, as not being quite so familiar to read as charts in which the lines are straight. Robust construction is a feature of this recorder.

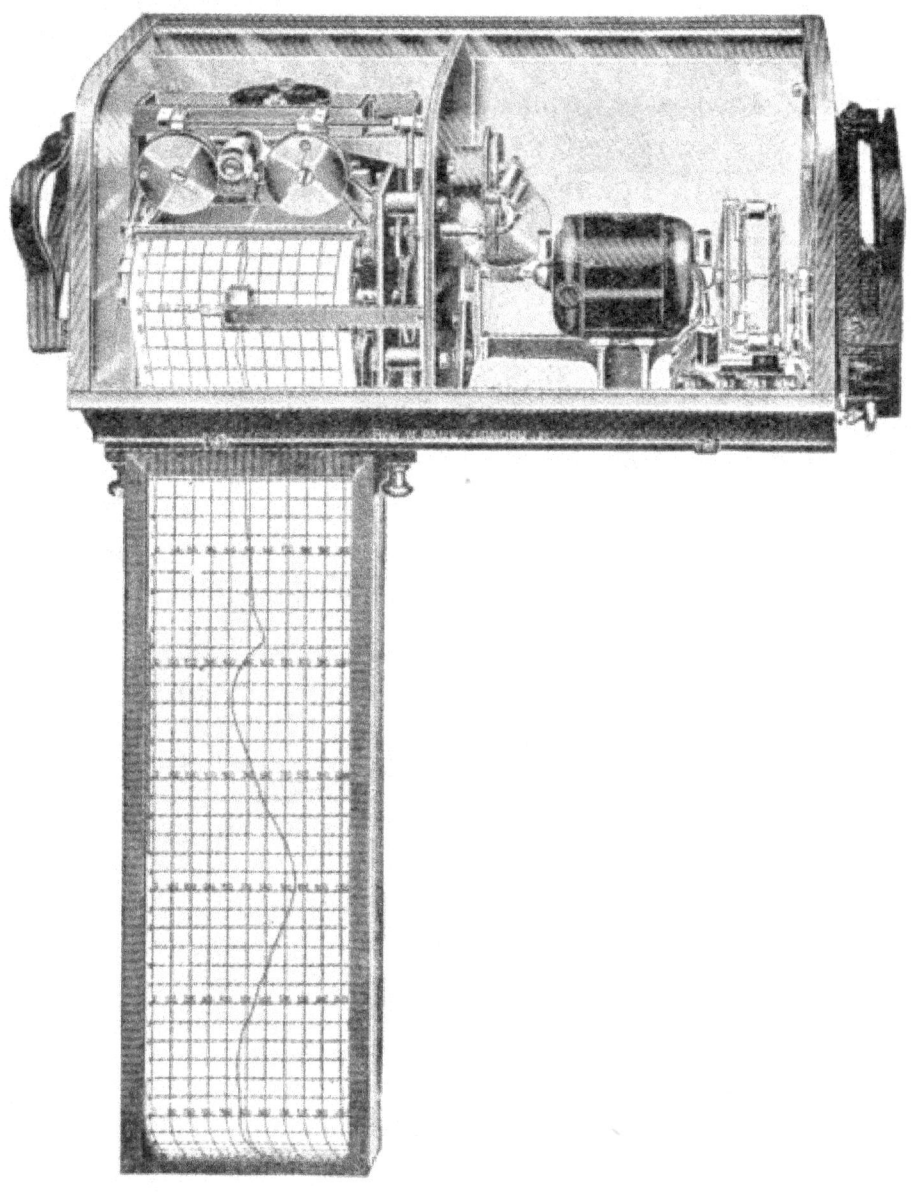

FIG. 25. PAUL'S RECORDER.

Paul's Recorder.—In the recorders previously described, the motive power is furnished by clockwork. R. W. Paul has introduced an instrument in which all the moving parts are actuated by a motor driven with power from the mains. This recorder is shown in fig. 25. The motor is furnished with a special type of governor to ensure constant speed, and is connected by suitable gearing to the mechanisms moving the chart, presser-bar, and inking ribbon, provision being made to vary the speeds of these movements by changing the gear. The galvanometer is of uni-pivot pattern, and the pointer is pressed at intervals on to a typewriter ribbon which lies above the chart. Immediately beneath the ribbon is placed a thin metal rod over which the paper passes, and the result of the contact is to produce a small dot. As in the thread recorder, the chart is divided into rectilinear coordinates, the ribbon in this case serving the same purpose as the thread in the former instrument. The lower part of the recorder is prolonged so as to display a considerable length of the chart, which is in the form of a roll, and is drawn forward by the mechanism. When two records are taken simultaneously the ribbon consists of two strips, one moistened with black ink, and the other with red; and it is arranged that each strip in turn is over the thin rod on to which the pointer is pressed, so that the records appear in separate colours. This recorder can also be arranged for multiple records, or fitted with a scale-control. With a view to workshop use, all the covers are fitted with faced metal joints, which are much better for keeping out dust than wooden ones. A further useful feature is that the various units in the recorder—galvanometer, motor, feed and record mechanism, and reducing gear—are all separate and interchangeable. By introducing a suitably divided chart this recorder will also serve for a radiation pyrometer, or, as will be shown later, for a resistance pyrometer.

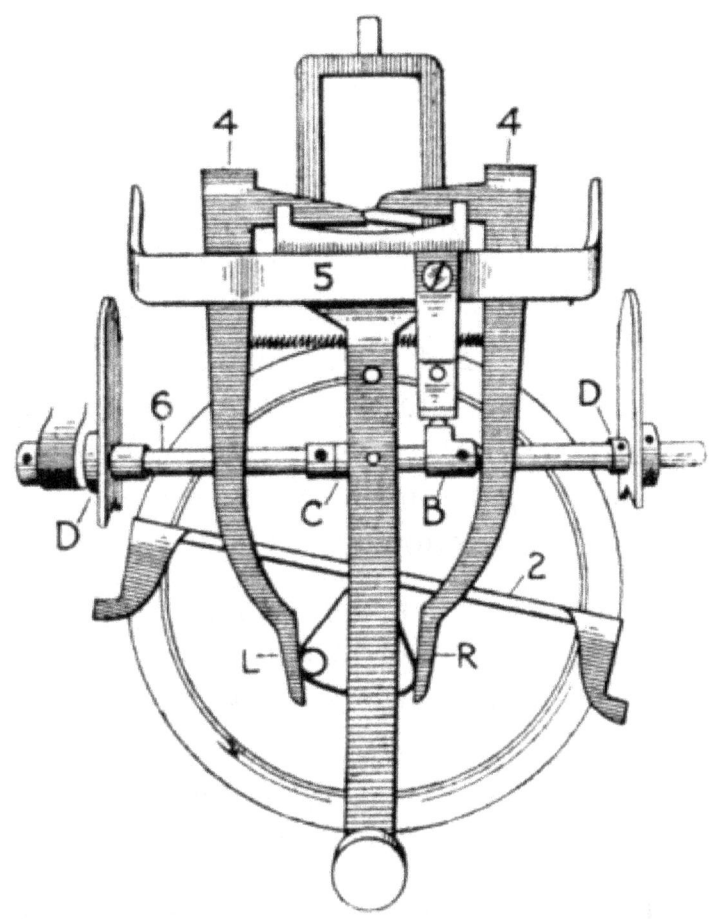

Fig. 26.—Leeds-Northrup Recorder.

The Leeds-Northrup Recorder.—The Leeds and Northrup Company, of Philadelphia, manufacture a recorder which is largely used in the United States. As in Paul's recorder, all the mechanism is motor driven; but the other arrangements are entirely distinct. Instead of measuring the deflection of the pointer, a zero deflection method is used. The pyrometer forms part of a potentiometer circuit, and the function of the mechanism is to oppose an E.M.F. equal to that of the pyrometer, from which the temperature is known. This has the advantage that the measurement is independent of the resistance of the leads, and is capable of great accuracy. The manner in which the adjustment of the opposing E.M.F. is controlled may be understood from fig. 26, in which the galvanometer coil is shown at the top of the figure. The shaft from the motor carries four cams, B, C, D, D, and at each revolution the cam B raises the bar (5) so as to press it against an arm attached to the galvanometer coil. At the same moment the cam C pushes against the bar (3), and thereby releases a clutch (2) from the disc beneath. As shown, the boom from the coil is to the right of the central position, and is gripped between a bar (5) and the lever (4) when the former rises, causing an angular movement of the clutch-arm (2). As the rotation continues the cam C leaves the bar (3), which then springs back and engages the clutch on the disc. The cam D then descends and presses on the projection of the clutch-arm to the left, causing the disc to rotate. The movement of the disc is conveyed to an arm which moves over the slide wire of the potentiometer; and this movement continues until the galvanometer boom is in the central or zero position, when neither of the levers 4, 4 is gripped, and consequently the disc is not fed in either direction. If the boom swing to the left, the movement of the disc will evidently be in the converse direction to that described.

In this recorder considerable power is available to drive printing or other mechanisms. The arm moving over the potentiometer wire carries a pen which marks the moving chart, or, when several records are taken simultaneously, a stamping machine is used which impresses the number of the pyrometer on the chart. The same galvanometer mechanism serves also for use with resistance pyrometers, as will be explained later.

Control of Furnace Temperatures.—Many attempts have been made to secure the automatic regulation of furnace temperatures by means of mechanisms controlled by an indicator or recorder. In the arrangement employed by the Brown Company of Philadelphia, movable stops are provided, which may be brought to any part of the scale, the mark between the stops representing the temperature it is desired to maintain. The indicator (or recorder) is provided with a presser-bar which descends periodically; and if the temperature be too low the depressed pointer completes a circuit through the inner stop, whilst if too high the circuit is through the outer stop. Both circuits contain a relay which brings a mechanism into operation, the result being to increase the supply of electricity or gas if the temperature be too low, or to diminish the supply when too high. When correct, the depression of the pointer fails to complete either circuit, and in this manner control between small limits may be ensured. In the case of large furnaces the relay circuits are employed to light lamps of different colours, the adjustment then being made by the man in charge of the furnace. Arrangements of this kind effect a considerable saving in fuel by preventing unnecessary heating, and are particularly valuable in cases where overheating would be deleterious to the articles in the furnace. The future will probably witness considerable developments along these lines.

Contact-Pen Recorders.—The force with which the pointer of an indicator is urged over the scale is relatively small, particularly in the case of pyrometers in which the platinum series of metals are used, as these furnish only a low E.M.F. If, therefore, the pointer terminate in a pen which is in continuous contact with the record-paper, the friction thus occasioned interferes considerably with the free movement of the pointer. When cheap-metal pyrometers are used, which yield a much higher E.M.F., the use of the pointer as contact-pen becomes more feasible, and if uniform friction at all parts of the paper can be ensured, records may be taken in this manner; and a recorder so constructed is simpler and cheaper than those of the intermittent type. Contact-pen recorders are used in America to some extent, being made by Bristol, Brown, and others; but so far British makers have not developed the manufacture of these instruments. At present, contact-pen recorders must be considered less accurate and reliable than those in which the contact is intermittent.

Installations of Thermo-electric Pyrometers.—When a number of furnaces in the same establishment are to be controlled, considerable economy may be effected by making one indicator serve for all the couples, which in this case must necessarily be made up of wires identical in thermo-electric value. Such an arrangement is shown in [fig. 27](), in which H^1 and H^2 represent two couples, one wire from each being connected to one of the terminals of the galvanometer G. The other terminal of the galvanometer is connected to the arm D of a switch, and the remaining thermocouple leads are connected to the points 1 and 2 respectively on the circumference. As shown, H^1 is connected to the galvanometer, and by turning the arm D to the point 2 the other couple would then be connected. Any number of junctions may thus be arranged with a single indicator. When this arrangement is adopted in a workshop, it is advisable to construct a small wooden building at a spot convenient for most of the furnaces, in which the indicator and switchboard are kept, and which could also contain a recorder if necessary; a spot as free as possible from vibration being preferable.

Separate indicators are only necessary when a furnace is used for special work.

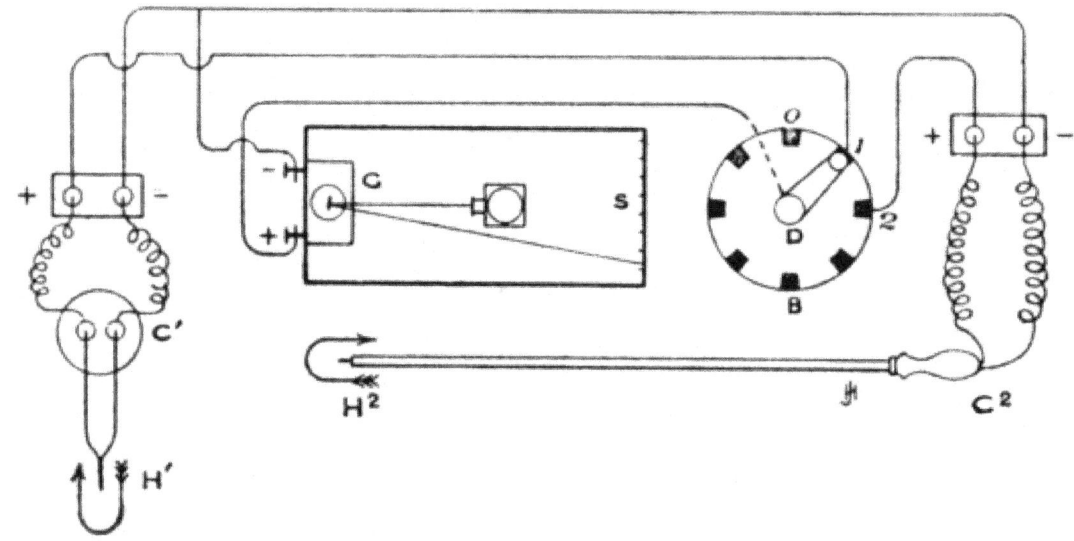

FIG. 27.—CONNECTIONS FOR AN INSTALLATION OF PYROMETERS.

In some instances a second indicator is kept in the shop office, to which all the pyrometers are wired, and which serves as a standard. The scale of the office indicator is checked daily at one point; and by connecting a given couple first with the shop indicator, and immediately afterwards with the office standard, any errors can be detected. It is also possible to ascertain the temperature of any given furnace in the office at any time, and so to control the whole. In fixing up such an arrangement it is necessary that each couple and its leads, up to the indicator, should possess the same resistance, or should not differ by an amount sufficient to affect the readings. The general experience of a properly managed installation is that the cost is saved in a few months in fuel alone; and, in addition, the work is carried out to much better advantage owing to complete control from the office.

Management of Thermo-electric Pyrometers.—Generally speaking, thermo-electric pyrometers give little trouble in practice, but the management should always be placed in skilled hands. It is advisable to test each instrument periodically at a fixed point near the working temperature, by the method explained on page 57; and if two or three pounds of material be used, the protecting shield need not be removed. A useful material for checking pyrometers near the critical range of steel is an alloy of 60 per cent. of copper and 40 per cent. of tin, which gives a well-defined freezing point at 738° C., and which may be used indefinitely in a reducing atmosphere Any serious error is easily detected by observing that the indications differ widely from those generally obtained under the same working conditions. If an error of 20° C. or more is noted, it is advisable to form a new junction, as the discrepancy will probably become greater, being due to a change at the hot junction. A small error, of the nature of 5 or 10° C., may be due to "creep" in the indicator, which may be adjusted accordingly, or a numerical correction may be made when taking a reading. An iron protecting sheath may be saved from rapid oxidation by black-leading once per week, which greatly prolongs its useful life, but should be replaced immediately it becomes dangerously thin in any part. Coating with aluminium powder also greatly prolongs the life of an iron sheath. When used in lead baths, the immersed part, if of iron or steel, should be bored from the solid, and left thick at the portion opposite the surface of the lead, where most corrosion occurs. A graphite tube, or one made of a composition containing graphite, is often useful in cases where iron is readily corroded, and can be used to much higher temperatures.

When a number of instruments are in use, it is advisable to keep a standard pyrometer for checking purposes, preferably one which has been certified by the National Physical Laboratory. In conducting a test, the couples, with protecting-tubes removed, may be placed in the tube of an electric furnace of the type shown in fig. 29, in close proximity with the standard junction. On raising the temperature gradually, the readings of each working instrument may be compared with the standard, and the necessary corrections discovered. Care must be taken to prevent contact with the furnace tube, and this may be accomplished by passing the wires through an asbestos stopper fitted into the end of the tube.

When recorders are used the attendant should make himself thoroughly conversant with the details of the mechanism, so as to be able to remedy any minor ailments, which are, as a rule, easily cured. On no account should an unskilled workman be trusted with recorders; it is better and safer to keep these in the office, where they will not be likely to be damaged or tampered with. All records should be kept for future reference, properly dated, and labelled according to the operations represented.

Laboratory Uses of Thermo-electric Pyrometers.—Numerous operations carried out in muffle furnaces at prescribed temperatures require no special precautions beyond those previously given. In determining the melting points of metals or alloys, however, a porcelain or silica sheath is inadvisable, as they are easily corroded. An iron sheath is proof against some metals, but not against others, and it is always safer to fix a thin fireclay sleeve, closed at the end, over the part immersed. A sheath of graphite or graphite composition may be used for temperatures above 1100° C.; and occasionally a sheath bored from a thick arc-lamp carbon, coupled to an iron tube beyond the heated part, will be found useful at high temperatures. Alundum is useful up to 1600° C, and for temperatures of this order the higher refractories such as silfrax and zirkite may also be used to advantage.

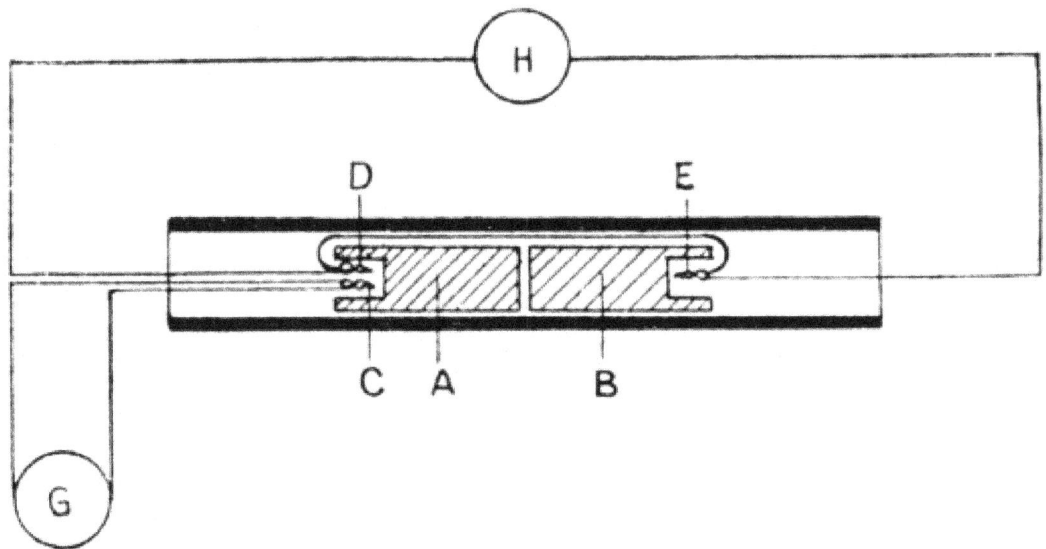

FIG. 28.—DIFFERENTIAL METHOD FOR DETERMINING CRITICAL POINTS OF STEEL.

The determination of the "critical" points of steel call for special mention. In cooling down a mass of steel the fall of temperature is arrested at one or more points, observations of which are frequently of service in deciding the subsequent treatment of the steel. A method commonly employed is known as the "differential method," and is indicated in fig. 28. The sample of steel, A, is placed side by side with a piece of nickel, B, of equal dimensions, in the tube of an electric furnace. A naked junction, C, is placed in a hole drilled in A, and is connected to the galvanometer G, which is calibrated to read temperatures. A two-junction circuit, formed of a junction D placed in the hole in A, and another junction E located in the hole in B, are connected to a delicate galvanometer H. The furnace is heated until the galvanometer G indicates 900° C., when the arrangement is allowed to cool. As A and B, under normal circumstances, cool at an equal rate, the junctions D and E will be at the same temperature, and no deflection will be observed on H. When, owing to recalescence, the cooling of A is arrested, B, not being thus affected, will continue to cool, thus producing a difference between the temperatures of D and E, and consequently a deflection on H. The temperature of A at the time this occurs is read off on G.

FIG. 29.—ELECTRIC TUBE-FURNACE.

The furnace illustrated in fig. 29 is suited to this determination. It consists of a silica tube 1 foot long, wound with a special resistance wire and efficiently lagged, and may be heated in safety to 1000° C. for long periods, and to 1200° for a short time. It may be placed across the electric mains directly, and reaches 900° C. in less than half an hour. It consumes 600 to 700 watts at the highest temperatures, and the cost of re-winding is small. This furnace is useful as a general laboratory appliance, and may be kept at a given steady temperature by the use of an external resistance.

The wires in this experiment should be platinum and iridioplatinum or rhodioplatinum, or a good pair of base metals, and the junctions in A should be separated from each other and from the specimen by asbestos; the same precaution being taken to prevent the junction E from touching B. A thin layer of mica should be used beneath A and B, to avoid contact with the furnace tube, which, when hot, allows of leakage of current from the heating coil. Both A and B may be 1½ in. long, ¾ in. diameter, with a hole ¼ in. diameter drilled to a depth of ¾ inch.

An alternative method is to insert a junction in a hole in the specimen, and to take direct readings as the temperature slowly rises or falls, when an arrest in the movement of the pointer of the indicator shows that the change-point has been reached. Special sets are made for this purpose.

Measurement of Lower Temperatures by the Thermo-electric Method.—Many cases arise in practice in which a thermal junction and a sensitive galvanometer are preferable to a mercury thermometer; and below -39° C., at which temperature mercury freezes, a thermal junction is frequently better to employ than an alcohol or pentane thermometer. A number of practical examples of the use of thermal junctions for ordinary and low temperatures will now be considered.

Measurement of Surface Temperatures.—A mercury thermometer, when laid on a hot surface, only touches along a line, and does not show the true surface temperature. The construction of a thermal junction suitable for this purpose is described on page 41, and for steam-pipe surfaces, hot plates, and the exterior of furnaces, a specially calibrated millivoltmeter, giving a full-scale deflection with 20 millivolts, may be used. In making the temperature scale, boiling water (100°C.), boiling aniline (184° C.), and melting tin (232° C.) are convenient standards. If the surface temperature be less than 100° C. a mirror galvanometer should be used, and the junction standardized in paraffin wax (freezing point usually about 50° C., but should previously be determined with an accurate thermometer), absolute alcohol at boiling point (79° C.) and boiling water. The author has found that this method yields excellent results in the case of steam-pipes, the exterior of rotary cement kilns, and hot surfaces generally.

Measurement of Low Temperatures.—Junctions of iron and constantan, Hoskin's alloys, copper and German silver, or copper and constantan, are suited to these measurements. In a laboratory the cold junction may be kept in ice in a Dewar vessel, the mechanically protected form known as the "Thermos" flask being very useful for this purpose. With a good mirror galvanometer precise readings may be secured, 1/10 of a degree C. being easily detected. Calibration between -40° and +40°C. may be effected by comparison with a standard mercury thermometer, a water-bath being used above 0°, and alcohol surrounded by a freezing mixture of ice and calcium chloride crystals below zero. For very low temperatures (-200°C. or less) the junction maybe calibrated in solid carbon dioxide (-78°C.) and liquid air (-184°C.). Dewar has found that copper and German silver form a reliable junction for very low temperatures, and the author has successfully used a couple of Hoskin's alloys for special work down to -200°C., a pivoted indicator being employed. No couples tested show a linear relation between E.M.F. and temperature at these low ranges.

Owing to the magnitude of the error caused by changes in the cold junction, the thermo-electric method is not suited to the measurement of atmospheric temperatures, or for explosive magazines or cold stores. In such cases instruments of the resistance type, to be described later, are used.

Temperature of Steam, Exhaust Gases, etc.—For measuring the temperature of ordinary or superheated steam, the exhaust gases from internal combustion engines, etc., iron-constantan junctions, with suitable indicators, are satisfactory. When placed in a pipe the junction should be as nearly as possible in the centre, so as to avoid the cooling effect of the walls. Several junctions, situated in different parts of the pipe, may be used with a single indicator and suitable switchboard. The above remarks also apply to the hot-blast for blast furnaces, and similar instances where the temperature does not exceed 900° C.

Measurement of Differences of Temperature.—Cases frequently arise in practice in which the difference in temperature between two points is required, and if this difference be subject to rapid changes, a mercury thermometer, from its large mass, would not respond with sufficient rapidity to indicate these changes. In such cases a circuit is made after the manner of fig. 2, one junction being located at each point; thin wires of iron and constantan being used. For small differences—1° C. or less—a mirror galvanometer should be used. Calibration may be performed by placing one junction in hot water and the other in cold, the water temperatures being read with an accurate thermometer.

Advantages of the Thermo-electric Method of Measuring Temperatures.—Compared with other methods, the thermo-electric possesses the following points of superiority:—(1) Simplicity, no special experiment being necessary to obtain a reading; (2) cheapness of outfit; (3) adaptability to a variety of purposes; (4) ease of repair in case of damage; (5) robustness, not being liable to get out of order under workshop conditions; and (6) suitability to the purpose of a centrally controlled installation. The drawbacks are:—(1) Liability to error owing to fluctuations in the cold junction (which may be avoided with care); and (2) lack of sensitiveness at very high temperatures compared with the resistance method—a point seldom of great practical importance, as the limit of accuracy is usually within the amount by which an ordinary furnace fluctuates in temperature under working conditions.

CHAPTER IV
RESISTANCE PYROMETERS

General Principles.—When a pure metal is heated, its resistance to electricity increases progressively with the temperature. Certain alloys, on the other hand, show a practically constant resistance at all temperatures, examples of such alloys being constantan, manganin, and platinoid. All the elementary metals, however, exhibit a tangible rise in resistance when the temperature is augmented; and Sir W. Siemens, in 1871, proposed to apply this principle to the measurement of high temperatures by determining the resistance, and deducing the corresponding temperature from a table prepared under known conditions.

The choice of a metal is in this case more greatly restricted than in the selection of materials for a thermal junction. A certain amount of external corrosion does not alter the E.M.F. of a junction; but an alteration in size produces a marked difference in the resistance of a wire, which varies directly as the length and inversely as the area of cross-section. To the necessity for the absence of any internal physical change affecting the resistance is therefore added the further condition of permanence of external dimensions. For temperatures above a red heat the only feasible metals to use are platinum or the more expensive metals of the platinum series—and hence platinum is universally employed for this purpose. The original Siemens pyrometer consisted of 1 metre of platinum wire, 1 millimetre in diameter, wrapped round a porcelain rod, and protected from furnace gases by an iron sheath An elaborate method of measuring the resistance, involving the electrolysis of acidulated water, was adopted for workshop use, but was too involved to become popular. Later, Siemens employed the differential galvanometer method, and finally the Wheatstone bridge, to measure the resistance. Both methods are still in use in connection with resistance pyrometers, and the principle of each will now be explained.

Measurement of Resistance by the Differential Galvanometer.—A differential galvanometer is one which possesses two windings, arranged so that a current passing through the one tends to turn the pointer in one direction, and through the other to cause a movement in the opposite direction. If the currents in each winding simultaneously be equal, the pointer remains at rest under the action of two equal and opposite forces. The experimental attainment of the condition of rest serves as a means of measuring resistance, the circuit being arranged as in fig. 30. Current from a battery B passes through a divided circuit, one branch containing the adjustable resistance R and one coil of the galvanometer G; and the other the unknown resistance P and the opposite coil. The resistance R is adjusted until on tapping the key K no deflection on the galvanometer is noted, when the current in each branch of the circuit will be the same. The resistances of each coil of the galvanometer being equal, it follows from Ohm's law that P is equal to R when no deflection is obtained.

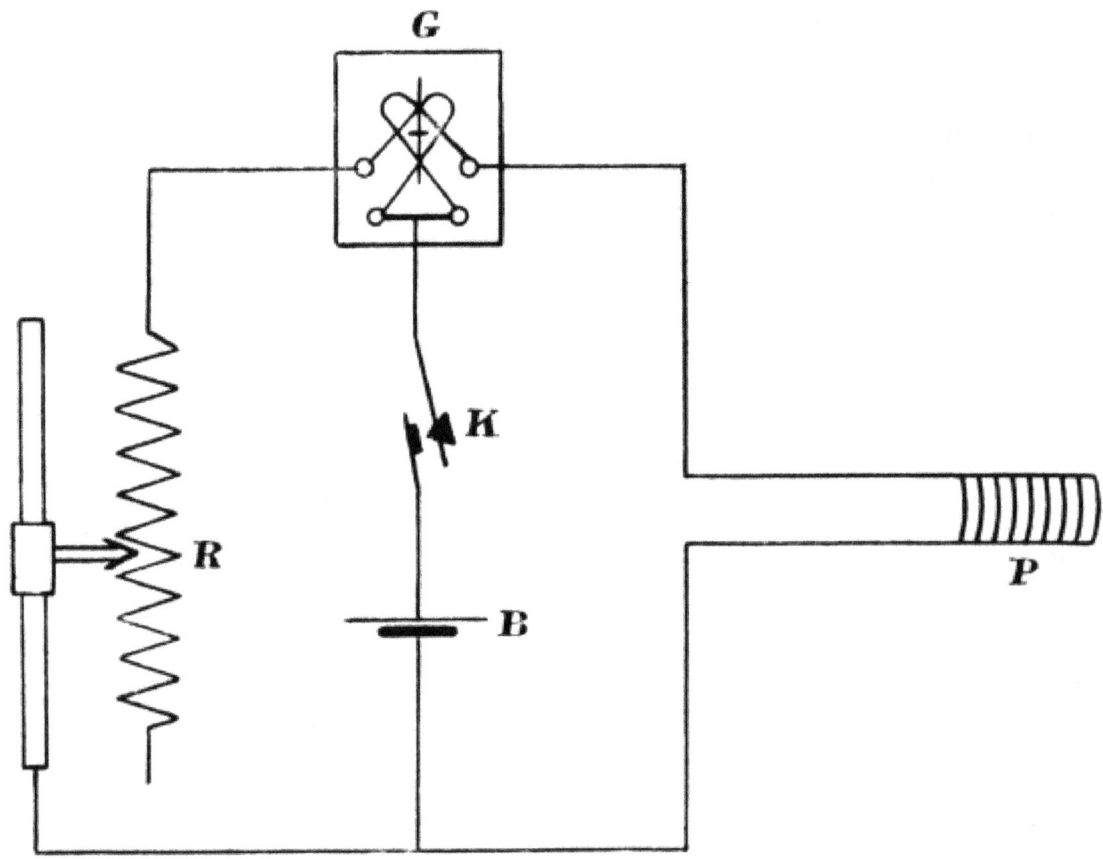

FIG. 30.—DIFFERENTIAL GALVANOMETER METHOD OF MEASURING RESISTANCE.

The accuracy of this method depends upon the sensitiveness of the galvanometer, and also upon the extent to which the two coils may be regarded as truly differential, as the measurement evidently assumes complete equality in resistance and effect on the moving part. With modern galvanometers of this pattern, it is possible to secure readings of sufficient accuracy for the purposes of pyrometry. The method, however, is less sensitive than the Wheatstone bridge, now to be described.

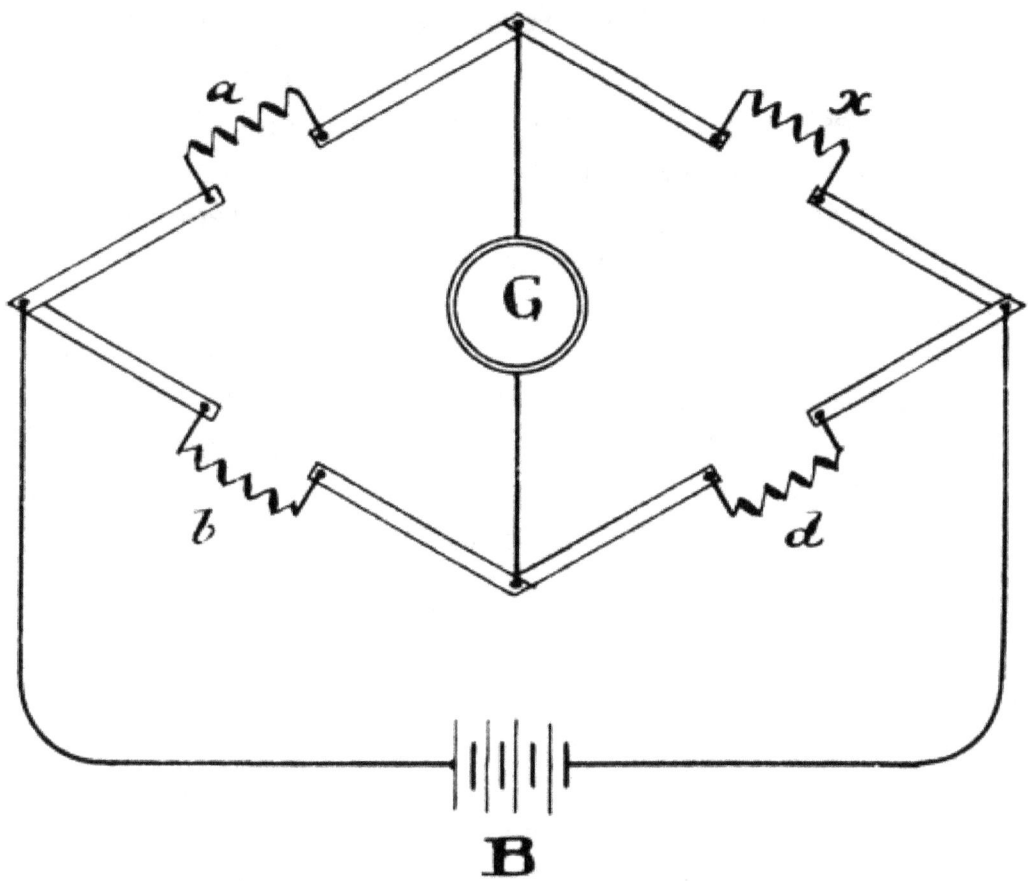

FIG. 31.—PRINCIPLE OF WHEATSTONE BRIDGE.

Measurement of Resistance by the Wheatstone Bridge.—The principle of this method is shown in fig. 31, where a and b are two fixed resistances of known value; d is an adjustable resistance; x the resistance to be measured; B a battery; and G a sensitive galvanometer. If, in this circuit, d be adjusted until no deflection is shown on the galvanometer, then $a/b = x/d$; or $x = (a \times d)/b$. Hence, if $a = b$, then x will be equal to d.

It is not difficult to construct a portable apparatus, suitable for workshop use, by means of which the value of x may be determined to 0·01 ohm; and in the laboratory, with a very delicate galvanometer, 0·001 ohm may readily be detected. The Wheatstone bridge method is the best for the accurate measurement of resistance; but in resistance pyrometers it is sometimes advisable to sacrifice extreme accuracy in order to gain advantages in other directions, as will be shown subsequently.

Relation between the Resistance of Platinum and Temperature.—As platinum is the only feasible metal to use in the construction of resistance pyrometers, it is essential that the effect of temperature on the resistance of this metal should be known. Difficulties were experienced, in the early days of resistance pyrometers, from the fact that different samples of platinum wire, of varying degrees of purity, gave widely differing results in this connection; and no certainty was attained until 1886, when Professor Callendar thoroughly investigated the subject, and evolved a formula from which the temperature of a given kind of platinum could be deduced with great accuracy from the resistance. In order to understand this formula and its application, it will be necessary to consider the underlying principles upon which it is founded.

If the resistance of a platinum wire be measured at a number of standard gas-scale temperatures, and the results depicted graphically by plotting resistances against corresponding temperatures, the curve obtained is part of a parabola, exhibiting a decrease in the rate at which the resistance increases at the higher temperatures. A second platinum wire, of different origin and purity, and of the same initial resistance as the foregoing, would furnish a curve which, although parabolic, would not overlap that obtained with the first wire. The advance made by Callendar was to deduce a formula from which the temperature of any kind of platinum wire could be deduced from its resistance, after three measurements at known gas-scale temperatures had been determined. The calibration of a resistance pyrometer was thereby reduced to three exact observations, instead of a large number distributed over the scale; and, moreover, the formula in question was found to give results of great accuracy over a wide range of temperature for any kind of platinum wire.

Before dealing with Callendar's formula, the term "degrees on the platinum scale" will be explained. Such degrees are obtained by assuming that the increase of resistance of platinum is uniform at all temperatures; that is, that the temperature-resistance curve is a straight line, and not a parabola. For example, a piece of platinum wire of 2·6 ohms resistance at 0° C. will show an increase to 3·6 ohms at 100° C.—an addition of 1 ohm for 100°. We now assume that a further augmentation of 1 ohm, bringing the total to 4·6 ohms, will represent an increase of 100°, or a temperature of 200°. Similarly, a total resistance of 5·6 ohms would indicate 300°, and 12·6 ohms 1000°. The temperature scale obtained by this process of extrapolation is called the "platinum scale," and differs considerably from the true or gas scale, the difference becoming greater as the temperature rises. This is indicated in fig. 32, in which A represents the true parabolic relation between resistance and temperature, and B the assumed straight-line relation. Reading from curve A, the temperature corresponding to 8 ohms resistance is 600° C.; but from B the same resistance is seen to represent only 545° C., which is the "temperature on the platinum scale" to which this resistance refers. An inspection of fig. 32 shows that at all temperatures, except between 0° and 100°, the platinum-scale readings for given resistances are less than those indicated on the gas scale.

Callendar's formula is expressed in terms of the difference between the gas-scale and platinum-scale readings, and takes the form

$$t - p = \delta \left\{ \left(\frac{t}{100}\right)^2 - \left(\frac{t}{100}\right) \right\}$$

where t = temperature on the gas scale,
p = temperature on the platinum scale.
δ = a constant, depending upon the purity of the wire.

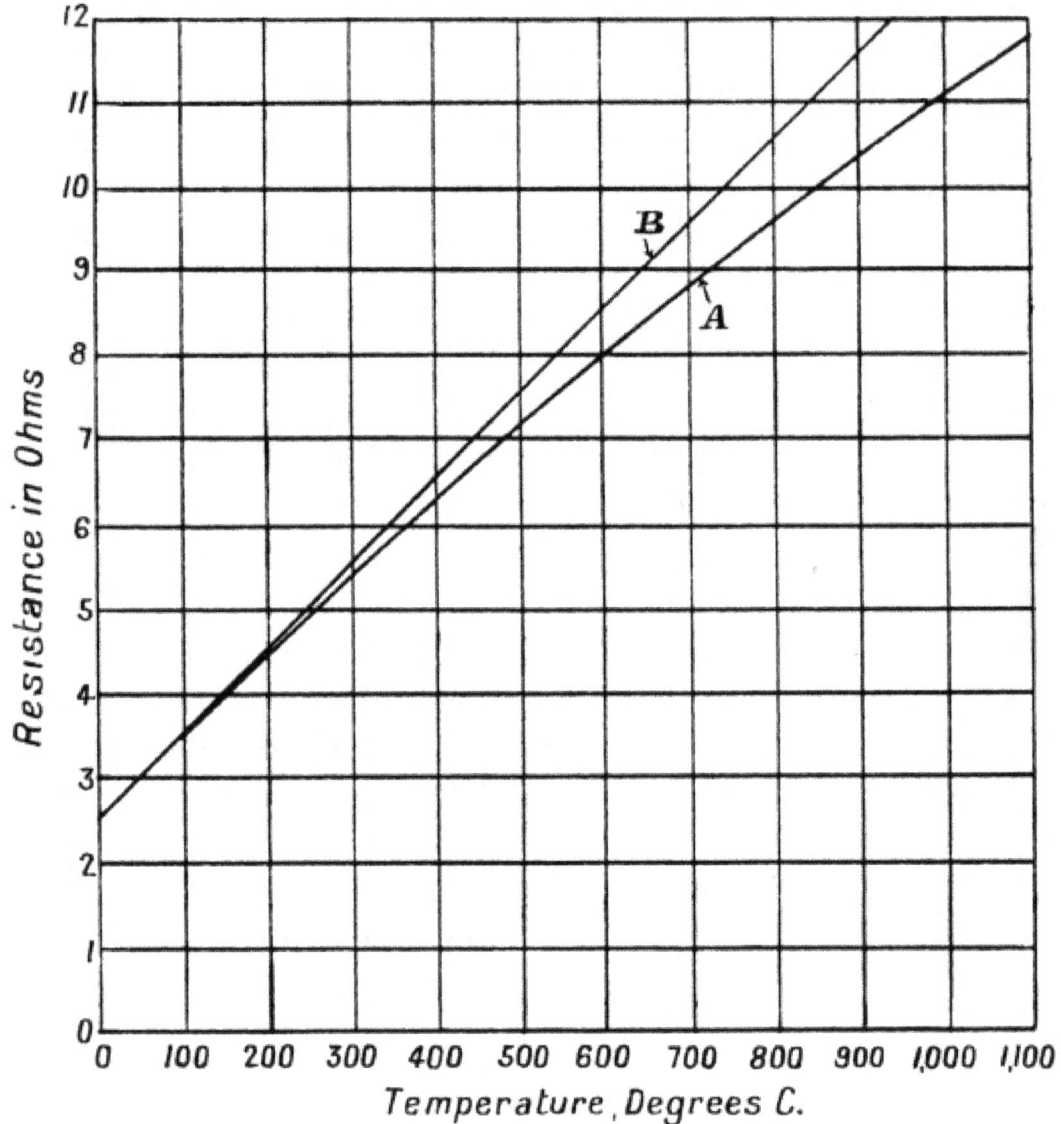

FIG. 32.—CONNECTION BETWEEN RESISTANCE OF PLATINUM AND TEMPERATURE:

A, ON GAS SCALE; B, ON PLATINUM SCALE.

In order to determine the value of δ, it is necessary to measure the resistance of the wire at 0°, 100°, and a third temperature, which should be considerably above 100°. The readings at 0° and 100° are requisite to establish the platinum scale of temperatures; the third reading is required to calculate the value of δ, as p and t are equal at 0° and 100°, these points forming the basis of both scales. An example is appended to make this matter clear.

Example.—A platinum wire has a resistance in ice of 2·6 ohms; in steam, 3·6 ohms; in boiling sulphur, 6·815 ohms. To find the value of δ, the boiling point of sulphur being 444·5 on the gas scale.

Since an increase of (3·6 - 2·6) = 1 ohm is produced by 100°, the increase observed in boiling sulphur, (6·815 - 2·6) = 4·215 ohms, will represent a temperature, on the platinum scale, of $(4·215 \times 100)/1 = 421·5°\ p$.

Applying Callendar's formula,

$$(444·5 - 421·5) = \delta \left\{ \left(\frac{444·5}{100}\right)^2 - \left(\frac{444·5}{100}\right) \right\}$$

the value of δ is found to be 1·5.

Callendar, in his experiments, employed the boiling point of sulphur for the third point, and determined this temperature on the gas scale with great accuracy, The necessity for extreme precision in applying this formula is made clear by noting the effects on the value of δ resulting from small differences in the figures chosen in the above example. If, for instance, the boiling point of sulphur on the gas scale were taken at 2° lower, or 442·5, the value of δ would work out to 1·37; and the error at 1200° C. thus caused would amount to 17°. The same discrepancy would be observed if the resistance in boiling sulphur were taken as 6·835 ohms, an error of 0·02 ohm; and a still greater error would result if the difference in resistance at 0° and 100° were measured as 0·99 ohm instead of 1 ohm. From an extensive experience of the difficulties attendant on correctly determining the value of δ, the author has found that no reliable result can be obtained unless measuring instruments of the highest precision are used, and elaborate precautions taken to ensure the exact correction for alterations in the boiling points of water and sulphur occasioned by changes in atmospheric pressure. Unless the necessary facilities are at hand, an operator would be well advised to standardize a resistance pyrometer by taking several fixed points and drawing a calibration curve, after the manner recommended for a thermo-electric pyrometer.

If a resistance pyrometer be calibrated so as to read in platinum-scale degrees, and the value of δ be known for the wire, the correct gas-scale temperatures may be calculated from Callendar's formula. The table on next page gives the results of a number of calculations made in this manner.

Changes in Resistance of Platinum when constantly Heated.
—The resistance of platinum undergoes a gradual change when the wire is kept continuously above a red heat; and if the temperature exceed 1000° C. the change becomes very marked after a time, leading to serious errors in temperature indications when used in a pyrometer. The alteration under notice is due, as shown by Sir William Crookes, to the fact that platinum is distinctly volatile above 1000° C., and hence the diameter of the wire diminishes. This variation constitutes a serious drawback to the use of resistance pyrometers for temperatures exceeding 1000° C.

COMPARISON OF GAS AND PLATINUM SCALES.
$\delta = 1\cdot 5$.

Platinum Thermometer Reading (Pt.).	Air Thermometer Reading t (deg. C.).	Difference (t - Pt.).
-100	-97·1	+ 2·9
0	0	0
50	49·6	- 0·04
100	100	0
200	203·1	3·1
300	309·8	9·8
400	420·2	20·2
500	534·9	34·9
600	654·4	54·4
700	779·4	79·4
800	910·7	110·7

900	1049·4	149·4
1000	1197·0	197·0
1100	1355·0	255·0
1200	1526·7	326·7
1300	1716·0	416·0

Terms used in Resistance Pyrometry.—Following on the researches of Callendar and others, certain terms relating to resistance pyrometers have come into use, and will now be defined.

(1) *The Fundamental Interval* is the increase in resistance between 0° C. and 100° C, or $R_{100}-R_0$. It should be remembered that the increases between 200° and 300°, or 800° and 900°, all temperatures being taken on the gas scale, differ from the fundamental increase.

(2) *The Fundamental Coefficient* is that fraction of the resistance at 0° C. by which it increases per degree between 0° and 100°, on the average, or

$$\frac{R_{100} - R_0}{R_0 \times 100}$$

This figure is in reality the average temperature coefficient between 0° and 100°. For pure platinum the value is or $1/260$ or 0·003846.

(3) *The Fundamental Zero* is the temperature, on the platinum scale, at which the resistance would vanish; it is evidently the reciprocal of (2), prefaced by a minus sign, or

$$-\frac{R_0 \times 100}{R_{100} - R_0}$$

For pure platinum this temperature would be -260p, since it is assumed that the average increase or decrease per degree holds throughout; that is, for every degree the metal is cooled the loss of resistance is taken to be 1/260 the resistance at 0°. Hence at -260p the resistance, on this assumption, would vanish.

(4) *The Difference Formula* is the expression which gives the relation between gas-scale and platinum-scale temperatures, or

$$t - p = \delta \left\{ \left(\frac{t}{100}\right)^2 - \left(\frac{t}{100}\right) \right\}$$

This formula has already been fully dealt with.

(5) *The Platinum Constant* is δ in the above expression. The value for pure platinum is about 1·5, but small quantities of impurities may alter the figure considerably. The truth of the formula (4), however, is unaffected by changes in δ, as p would be correspondingly altered.

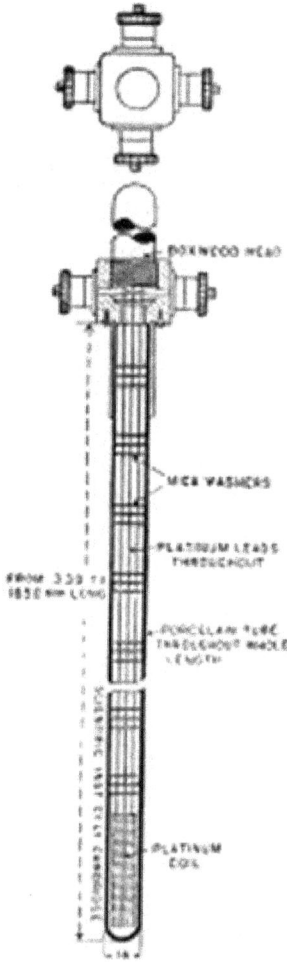

Fig. 33.—Platinum Resistance Pyrometer.

Practical Forms of Resistance Pyrometers.—A typical form of resistance pyrometer, made by the Cambridge and Paul Instrument Company, is illustrated in fig. 33. The coil of platinum wire is wound round the edges of a mica framework, made of two strips of mica fastened at right angles so as to form a + in section. This method of winding is due to Callendar, who discovered that mica was chemically inert towards platinum, even at high temperatures. The leads, also of platinum wire, pass from the coil through mica washers to terminals fastened to the boxwood head. A second wire, not connected with the coil, but identical in length and diameter with the ordinary leads, is bent into two parallel branches, which are passed through the mica washers side by side with the leads, and are brought to a second pair of terminals in the head. The function of this wire is to compensate for changes in the resistance of the leads when heated, by opposing the compensating wire to the pyrometer in the measuring arrangement, when the resistance of the leads and wire, being equal, will cancel, the resistance actually measured being in consequence that of the coil only. Fig. 34 shows the connections for a Wheatstone bridge when this method of compensation is employed, a and b representing two equal fixed resistances, P the pyrometer coil, x the leads, L the compensating wire, and d the adjustable resistance. When no deflection is observed on the galvanometer,

$$a/b = (x + P)/(L + d)$$

and since $a = b$ and $x = L$, it follows that $P = d$.

The protecting tube used by the Cambridge and Paul Instrument Company is made of porcelain, which is found to shield the platinum completely from the furnace gases, but is extremely fragile, and for workshop use should be protected by an outer iron sheath.

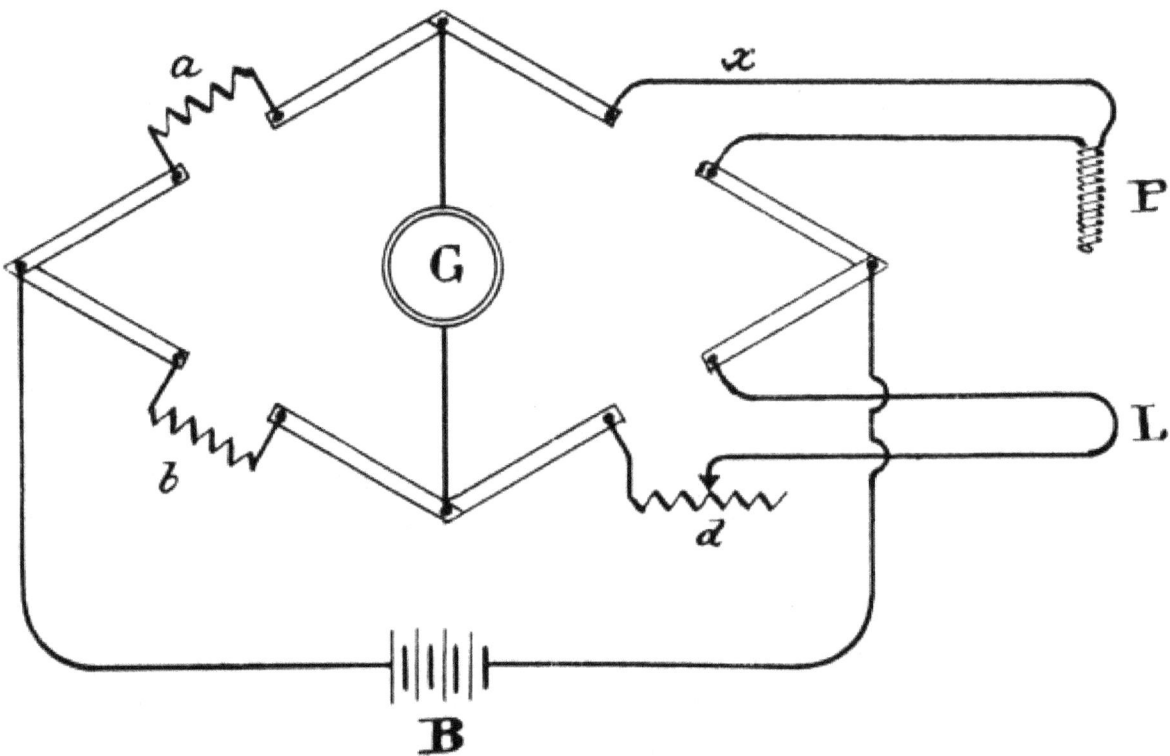

FIG. 34.—WHEATSTONE BRIDGE AS USED WITH A RESISTANCE PYROMETER.

Resistance pyrometers made by other firms differ in detail from the foregoing. In the Siemens pyrometer the coil is wound on special fireclay, and protected by an iron sheath, the space between the coil and the sheath being filled with magnesia, which effectively prevents the corrosion of the platinum; and compensation is effected by means of a single wire passing down the centre and connected to one end of the coil, a special form of Wheatstone bridge being used to take the measurement. In the instruments made by R. W. Paul the coil is made of flat strip rolled out from wire, wound on mica, and protected by a silica tube and outer iron sheath. The Leeds-Northrup Company of Philadelphia employ a rod of obsidian on which to wind the coil, and also make a form in which the coil is wound so as to be self-sustaining, thus dispensing with the support. In all cases the coil is wound non-inductively, *i.e.* the wire is doubled before making into a spiral.

The zero resistance of a given instrument depends upon the accuracy of the measuring appliances used, and upon the degree of precision it is desired to attain. If, for example, it is intended to read to 1°C., with appliances capable of measuring to 1/100 of an ohm, a convenient zero resistance is 2·6 ohms; it being found that with pure platinum the resistance rises from 2·6 ohms at 0° to 3·6 ohms at 100° C., an increase of 1/100 of an ohm for 1° C. With coarser measuring arrangements, for the same degree of precision, a correspondingly higher zero resistance will be required; thus if 1/25 ohm be the least amount detectable by the measuring device, a zero resistance of 10·4 ohms would enable 1° C. to be observed. It is evident that a suitable zero resistance may be calculated similarly in all cases when the limit of the measuring appliance is known, and the minimum temperature interval specified.

For work above a red heat, the leads from the coil should always be made of platinum. Copper leads, when heated, give off vapour in sufficient quantity to attack the platinum; and the same applies to a greater degree to all kinds of solder. For low temperature work, however, copper leads may be used, thus reducing the cost of the instrument. Mica, above 1000° C., tends to crumble; and most forms melt at 1300° C. or lower; hence a mica-wound instrument should not be used continuously above 1000° C. The fireclay winding used by Siemens permits of occasional readings being taken up to 1400° C., and the same applies to wires wound on obsidian (melting point = 1550° C.), or those in which the coil is self-sustaining. As previously mentioned, however, alterations in the platinum itself render continuous readings above 1000° C. inaccurate after a short time.

It has been pointed out that with accurate measuring devices, a resistance corresponding to a change of 1° C. can be measured; and it might appear at first sight that the resistance method is considerably more accurate in practice than the thermo-electric. If a perfectly constant temperature were to be measured, a resistance pyrometer would undoubtedly give a closer indication; but constancy to 10° C. is seldom possible with gas-fired or coal furnaces or other hot spaces in which pyrometers are used. The accuracy of a pyrometer under workshop conditions therefore depends upon the rapidity with which it responds to temperature fluctuations, which condition will evidently be influenced by the thermal conductivity of the sheath. As it is necessary to protect a resistance pyrometer with a porcelain or silica sheath, both of which are poor conductors of heat, this instrument is in consequence not capable of following a rapidly changing temperature. The same applies to the magnesia packing used in the Siemens form; whereas a thermo-electric pyrometer is often sufficiently shielded by an iron tube, which transmits heat with a fair degree of freedom. The superior delicacy of the resistance method is therefore nullified by the sluggishness of its indications; and for reading changing temperatures the thermo-electric pyrometer is at least equally accurate. If, however, a constant temperature can be obtained, as in the determination of melting points, or when using experimental furnaces capable of exact regulation, the steady temperature reading may be secured with greater precision by using the resistance pyrometer.

Indicators for Resistance Pyrometers.—All existing indicators for resistance pyrometers are in reality outfits for measuring resistance, either by the Wheatstone bridge, differential galvanometer, or other method, the resistance being translated on the dial into corresponding temperatures. Typical examples will now be described.

Fig. 35.—Siemens' Dial Indicator.

Siemens' Indicator.—This instrument is based upon the Wheatstone bridge principle, and is shown in fig. 35. The galvanometer is mounted in the centre of the dial, round the edge of which is fixed a ring on which the adjustable resistance is wound in spiral form. Suitable terminals are provided, duly labelled, to which the battery, pyrometer leads, and compensator are attached. A brass arm, movable about the centre of the dial, terminates in a tapping-key which moves over the adjustable resistance; the key being placed in the battery circuit. The fixed known resistances are located in the interior of the indicator. The adjustment consists in moving the key round the circumference until, on tapping, no deflection is obtained on the galvanometer. The pointed end of the movable arm then indicates the temperature of the pyrometer on the dial, which is marked in temperatures corresponding to the resistance opposed to the pyrometer for different positions of the key. In taking a reading, the operator is guided by the fact that when the temperature indicated is too high, the movement of the galvanometer needle will be in one direction; whereas if too low an opposite deflection will be given. The intermediate position of no deflection must then be found by trial; and the procedure should not occupy more than two minutes if the observer possess an approximate notion of the temperature to be measured.

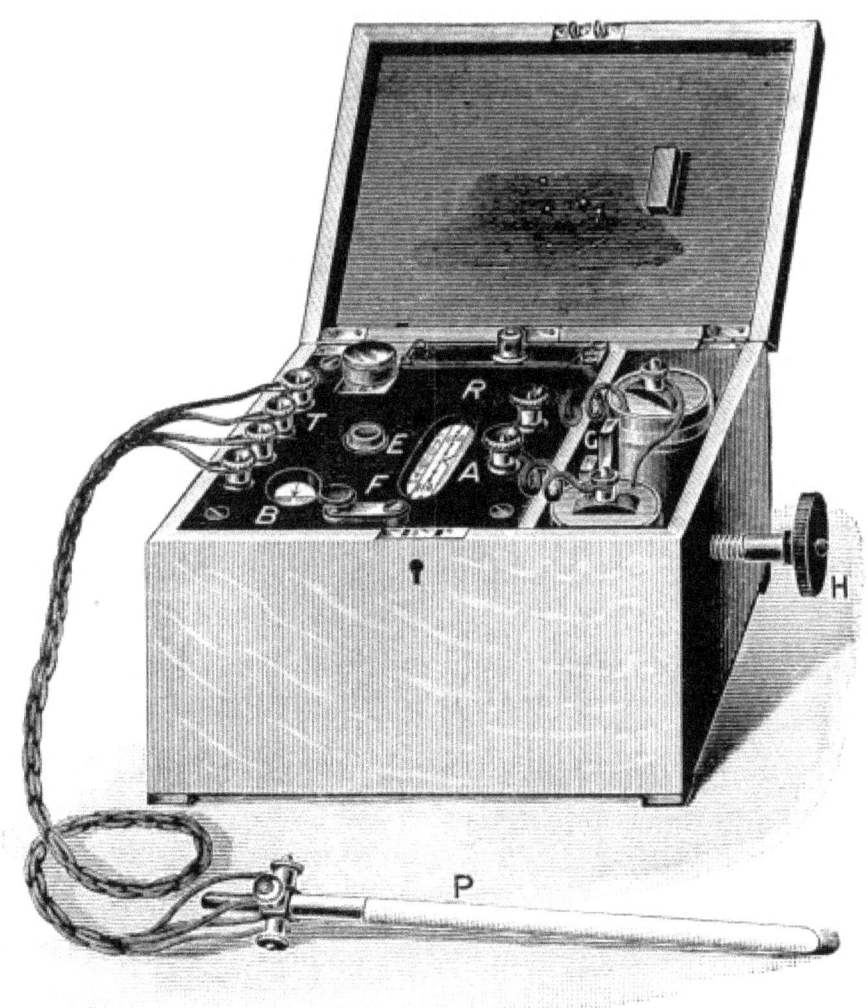

Fig. 36—Whipple's Indicator.

Whipple's Indicator.—This instrument (fig. 36) is employed by the Cambridge and Paul Instrument Company, and is also a form of Wheatstone bridge. The pyrometer leads and compensator are connected to properly labelled terminals T, and the battery to other terminals at the opposite side of the box. The pointer of the galvanometer is visible through the small window B, and a battery of two dry cells is placed at the side of the box.

The fixed resistances are contained in the interior, and the adjustable resistance consists of a continuous wire wound on a drum, which may be rotated by the handle H. The shaft connecting H with the drum is screwed, and works in a nut, so that the turning of H produces a spiral movement of the drum. The adjustment consists in rotating H until, on tapping the key F, no deflection of the galvanometer pointer is observed. The temperature of the pyrometer is then read off directly from a paper scale wound round the drum and rotating with it, visible through the window A, the reading being indicated by a fixed pointer. This arrangement forms a compact and convenient indicator.

FIG. 37.—THE HARRIS INDICATOR.

The Harris Indicator.—In the Siemens and Whipple indicators it is necessary, before a reading can be taken, to adjust a resistance until the galvanometer shows no deflection—an operation which takes up time and requires a fair amount of skill. This is obviated in the Harris indicator, made by R. W. Paul, and shown in fig. 37. This instrument is a special form of ohmmeter, which automatically indicates the resistance of the pyrometer by the movement of the pointer; the scale, however, being divided so as to read corresponding temperatures. In this indicator the scale may be made to notify an excess temperature—say 100°—above a given fixed number, and hence is capable of yielding an exact reading over the working range for which it is used. It may also be connected so that the whole scale represents the complete range—say 0° to 1000° C.—or other specified interval. The advantage possessed by this instrument is that the manipulation is much simpler than in the indicators previously described.

The Leeds-Northrup Indicator.—In this apparatus the Wheatstone bridge principle is employed, but the galvanometer is provided with a scale divided or temperatures. Coils are provided which correspond to an increase of resistance due to a rise of 100° C. on the part of the pyrometer, and by inserting these coils in the circuit the temperature is obtained to the nearest 100°. If the temperature were exactly at an even hundred—say 700°—the pointer of the galvanometer would be at zero on its scale; but if now the temperature rose, the system would no longer be balanced, and the galvanometer pointer would move over its scale by an amount depending upon the potential difference at its terminals. A very sensitive galvanometer would give a movement to the end of its scale with a slight alteration from the correct balance of the system; but by using a coarser instrument the pointer would remain within bounds; and the greater the increase of resistance, the larger would be the deflection. It is possible, in such a case, to divide the galvanometer scale to read temperatures corresponding to a given increase above that of the coils placed in the circuit. In one form of the Leeds-Northrup indicator, the whole scale is thus divided to read 100°, and the reading is obtained by adding the figure shown on the galvanometer to the hundreds represented by the coils inserted. In another form the galvanometer has a central zero, and its scale is divided both right and left, one side giving the number of degrees above, and the other below, the nearest hundred. The observations are thus much simpler than in the case where adjustment to the condition of no deflection is requisite.

Siemens' Differential Indicator.—This form of indicator is still in use, and consists of a differential galvanometer and box of resistance coils, connected as shown in [fig. 30](). By adjusting the coils until no deflection is produced, the resistance of the pyrometer is obtained, and the corresponding temperature read off from tables provided. This form of indicator is preferred by some users, but it is less sensitive than the more recent Wheatstone bridge indicator made by this firm (fig. 35), and equally difficult to manipulate.

Recorders for Resistance Pyrometers.—The value of records in high-temperature work has led to the invention of recording mechanisms for use with resistance pyrometers. The form in common use in Britain is that devised by Callendar, shown in fig. 38, and consists of a mechanism for restoring automatically the balance of the resistances in a Wheatstone bridge circuit, in such a manner as to indicate the existing resistance on a chart. To this end the moving coil of the galvanometer carries a boom, or contact-arm, which, on swinging to the right or left, completes one of two electric circuits. The closing of either circuit brings into action a clockwork mechanism, which causes a slider carrying a pen to move over the bridge wire until the balance is restored, and incidentally to produce a mark in ink on a paper wound on a drum, which rotates at a known speed. When the resistance of the pyrometer is balanced, the galvanometer boom will be in a central position, and the slider at rest; whereas a rise in temperature causing an increase in the resistance of the pyrometer, will result in the boom swinging over and completing the circuit, which introduces more resistance in opposition to the pyrometer. A fall in temperature will similarly result in the liberation of the second mechanism, owing to the boom swinging in the opposite direction, with the result that the slider moves so as to oppose a less resistance to the pyrometer. If the chart be divided horizontally into equal spaces, representing equal increments or decrements of resistance, they may be marked to represent degrees on the platinum scale, which may be translated into ordinary degrees by reference to a conversion table. In careful and skilled hands this recorder gives excellent results, and the value of the records obtained is clearly shown by an inspection of the example shown in fig. 39, which represents the fluctuations of an annealing furnace during a period of nine hours. It will be noted that during the period covered by workman A the furnace has received constant and careful attention; but workman B has evidently neglected his duty conspicuously at two separate times.

FIG. 38.—CALLENDAR'S RECORDER.

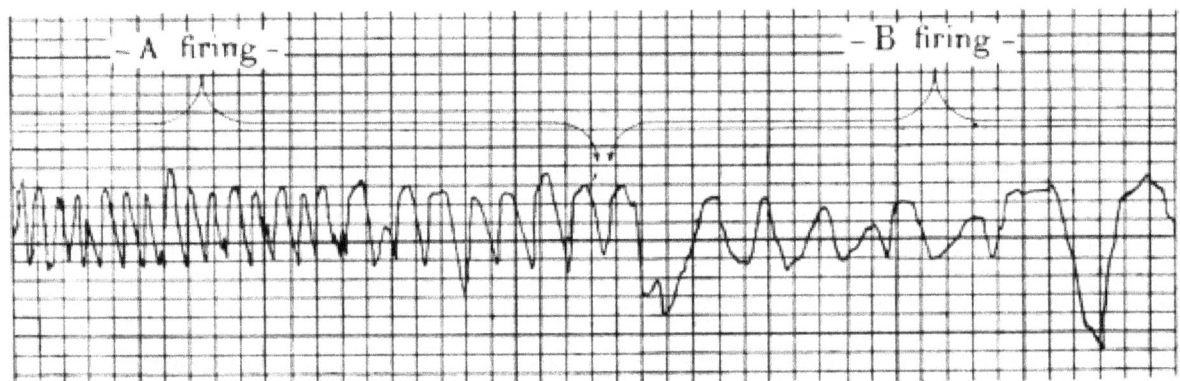

FIG. 39.—RECORD OBTAINED WITH CALLENDAR'S RECORDER.

The Leeds-Northrup Recorder.—In the Callendar recorder the boom which completes the electric circuits is pressed against the contact-surface merely by the small force due to the axial twist of the galvanometer coil, which necessitates the use of delicate mechanism if certainty of action is to be secured. A surer contact is secured in the instrument made by the

Leeds-Northrup Company of Philadelphia, by means of an intermittent action which will be understood from the annexed drawing (fig. 40). The boom from the galvanometer terminates in a platinum tip, P, which moves between two blocks, the upper of which consists of two pieces of silver, A and B, separated by a strip of ivory, I, whilst the lower block, C, is another piece of silver, which is moved periodically up and down by an electro-magnetic contrivance not shown in the drawing. When the galvanometer is at the position of balance, the tip of the boom is beneath the ivory piece I; and when C ascends the tip P is then squeezed on to the ivory, and no current will then pass from the battery through either of the circuits E or F. If, however, the point of the boom be beneath A, owing to an alteration in the temperature of the pyrometer, then on C rising the circuit through E will be completed; and, similarly, if beneath B the circuit through F will be established. The result in either case is to bring into action a mechanism which moves a slider, carrying a pen, over a resistance wire opposed to the pyrometer in such a manner as to restore the balance. Certainty of contact is thus secured, which enables all the parts to be strongly made. The actual recorder is shown in fig. 41, in which it will be seen that the slider carries an ordinary stylographic pen in contact with the chart. This recorder is worked on the differential galvanometer method; and the adjusting resistance, over which the slider moves, consists of a manganin wire wound on a tapered core, such that horizontal movements represent equal changes of temperature, and not of resistance, thus obviating the necessity of translating platinum-scale readings into ordinary degrees. Concordant and accurate results, coupled with robust construction, are claimed for this instrument by the makers. The other type of recorder made by this firm (fig. 26) may also be used in conjunction with a resistance pyrometer. In this case the movements described introduce or cut out resistance opposed to the pyrometer in a Wheatstone bridge circuit, until the balance is restored.

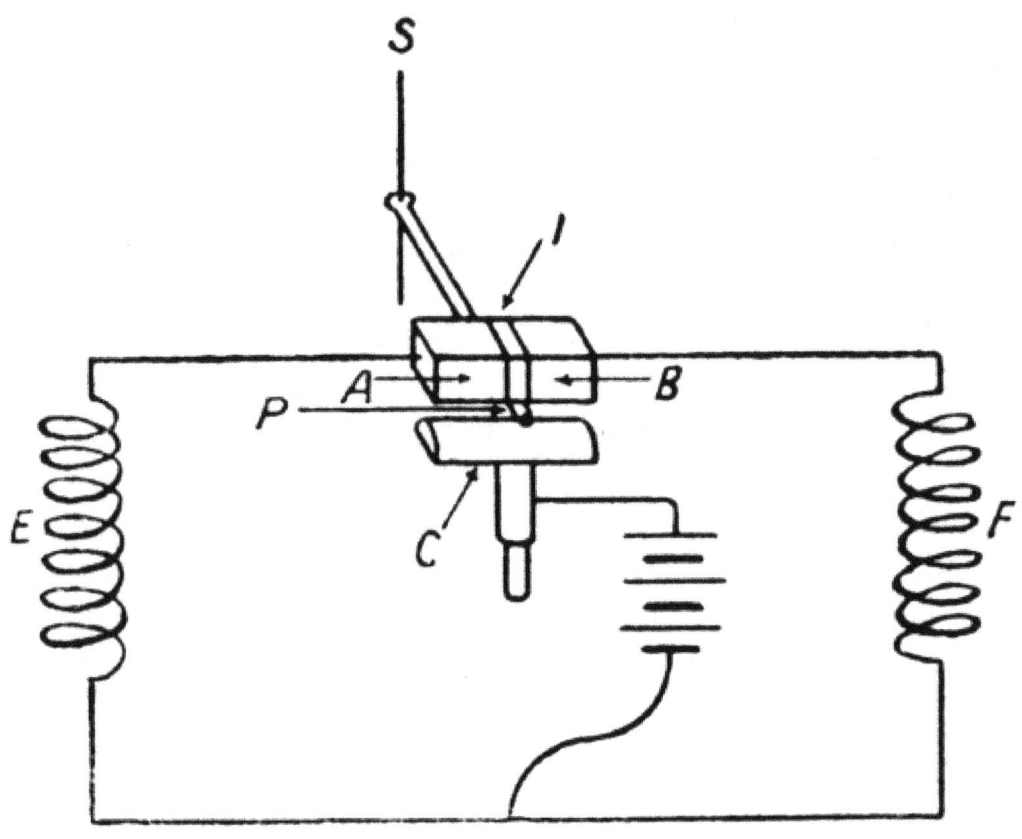

Fig. 40.—Principle of Leeds-Northrup Recorder.

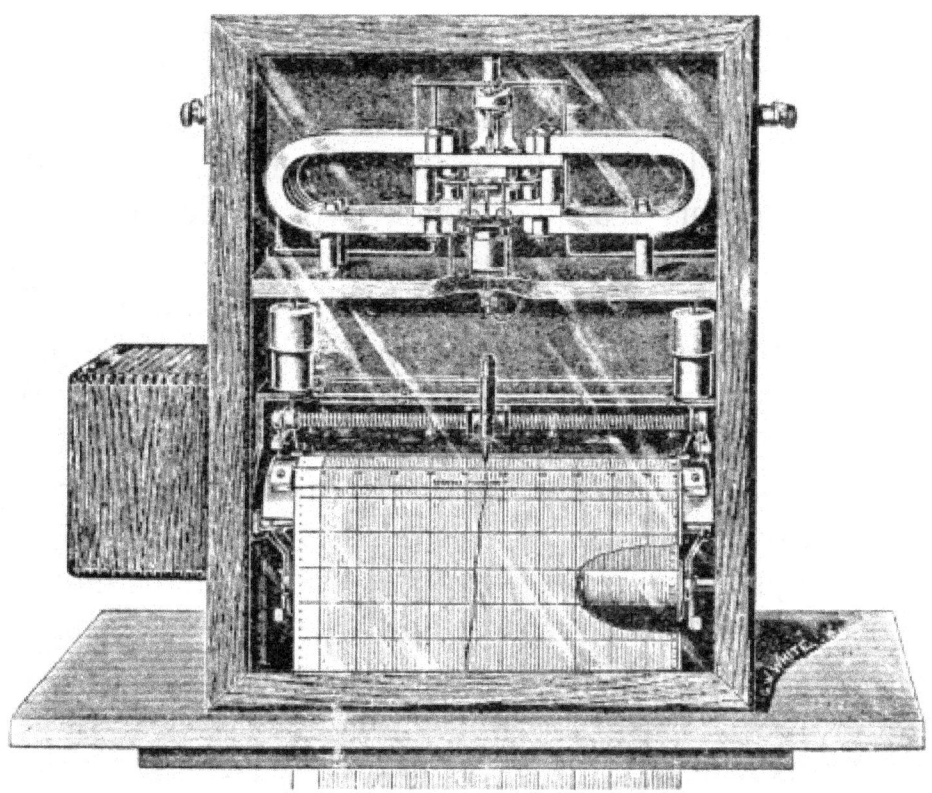

Fig. 41.—Leeds-Northrup Recorder.

Paul's Recorder.—This instrument, as used for thermo-electric pyrometers, has already been described. By replacing the galvanometer by a Harris indicator, and using a suitable chart, the same mechanism serves to record the indications of a resistance pyrometer.

Installations of Resistance Pyrometers.—The resistance method cannot be so readily applied to the purpose of a centrally controlled installation as the thermo-electric, owing to the difficulty of producing a set of pyrometers exactly equal in resistance. The introduction of the ohmmeter method of measuring resistances, as in the Harris indicator (page 122), has, however, rendered this project feasible, as it is possible in this arrangement to bring a set of pyrometers to a common resistance by adding the requisite amount in the form of a wire of negligible temperature coefficient. Several instruments, brought thus to a zero resistance of 3 ohms, for example, may then be wired up to a Harris recorder, and will give closely identical results. For various reasons, however, a thermo-electric installation is preferable.

Management of Resistance Pyrometers.—It is not advisable to use resistance pyrometers continuously above 900° C. (1650° F.), although an occasional reading may be taken up to 1200° C. (2190° F.). Great care must be taken that metallic vapours or furnace gases do not find access to the interior, and for this reason a cracked or defective sheath should immediately be replaced. As the resistance gradually changes, even when 900° C. is not exceeded, a reading should be checked at a fixed point in the neighbourhood of the working temperature, and allowance made for the observed error. Another method of correction recommended by some makers is to measure the resistance in ice, and to note how much this differs from the zero resistance noted when the indicator was marked, and to correct by simple proportion. Thus, if the observed resistance in ice were 10·2 ohms, the original having been 10·0 the reading on the indicator would be multiplied by $10·0/10·2 = 0·98$, a correction which assumes a linear relation between resistance and temperature, and is therefore only approximate. Generally speaking, any serious defect entails the sending of the instrument to the maker, as a special degree of skill is required to execute the necessary repairs.

As the indicators are usually not automatic in action, care should be taken in the manipulation not to damage any part, particularly the galvanometer; and it is advisable not to trust the instruments to unskilled observers. The remarks applying to recorders and protecting sheaths in relation to thermo-electric pyrometers (page 92) apply equally in this case.

Special Uses of Resistance Pyrometers.—In all cases in which an exact reading is required, and a steady temperature can be secured, the resistance pyrometer can be used to advantage. Thus for accurate determinations of melting points and boiling points, or for exact readings of temperatures in experimental furnaces, a resistance pyrometer is superior to appliances of other kinds. On the other hand, it is not capable of responding to changes with the same rapidity as a thermal junction, and is therefore inferior for such purposes as the determination of recalescence points, or the temperature of exhaust gases from an internal combustion engine. The resistance method may be applied to atmospheric and very low temperatures (liquefied gases, etc.), to measure steady conditions with accuracy, nickel wire being sometimes used instead of platinum below 400° C. Many cold stores are fitted with resistance thermometers, the temperature being read directly on the galvanometer, which is placed across a Wheatstone bridge, and shows a deflection which depends upon the amount by which the bridge is thrown out of balance. Changes in the temperature of the resistance element may thus be read accurately. Whether the resistance method is suitable to a given purpose must be decided by the three factors: (1) temperature to be measured, which must not exceed 1000° C. continuously; (2) degree of accuracy required (a thermo-electric pyrometer giving results to 10° C.); (3) stability of the temperature measured, rapid changes not being readily shown by resistance pyrometers.

One advantage of resistance pyrometers is that the readings are independent of the resistance of the wires used to connect the pyrometer with the indicator, as such wires are duplicated and opposed to each other in the measuring device, their resistance being thereby cancelled. Hence the same reading is obtained at any distance, and, in addition, the head of the pyrometer may vary in temperature to any extent without altering the reading. These are points of superiority over the thermo-electric method; but, on the other hand, resistance pyrometers and indicators are more costly, more fragile, more difficult to repair, require more skilled attention, and are more liable to get out of order when used for industrial purposes. These drawbacks have resulted in restricting the use of resistance pyrometers to special purposes, the general run of observations being conducted by means of thermo-electric pyrometers.

CHAPTER V
RADIATION PYROMETERS

General Principles.—It is a common experience that the heat radiated by a substance increases as its temperature rises; and it would obviously be an advantage if the temperature of a hot body could be deduced from the intensity of its radiations, as the measurement could then be made from a distance, without the necessity of placing a pyrometer in contact with the heated substance. At temperatures above 1000° C., when difficulties are experienced either with the metals or protecting sheaths of thermo-electric or resistance pyrometers, the advantage gained would become more conspicuous as the temperature increased. A brief survey of our knowledge of the relations between radiant energy and temperature will indicate how this desired end may be achieved.

Any substance at a temperature above absolute zero (-273° C.) radiates energy to its surroundings by means of ether waves. Below 400° C. these waves produce no impression on the retina of the eye, and the radiating body is therefore invisible in a dark room. Above 400° C., however, a proportion of visible waves are emitted; and as the temperature rises the effect on the retina is enhanced, and the body increases in brightness. The difference between the non-luminous and luminous waves is merely one of wave-length, the shorter wave-lengths being visible to the eye; and both represent radiant energy. In addition to giving out radiant energy, a substance receives waves from its surroundings, which it absorbs in greater or less degree, and which when absorbed tend to raise the temperature of the receiving substance. A number of objects in a room, all at the same temperature, are therefore radiating energy to one another, and equality of temperature is established when each object receives from its surroundings an amount of energy equal to that which it radiates. A hot substance radiates more energy than a cold one; thus if a hot iron ball be hung in a room it will radiate more energy to its surroundings than it receives from them, and will therefore cool until the outgoing energy is balanced by the incoming, when its temperature will be equal to that of the other objects in the room.

The rate at which a substance emits or takes up radiant energy depends upon the nature of its surface. A rough, black surface, such as may be obtained by holding an object in the smoke from burning camphor, radiates and absorbs heat with greater freedom than any other; whilst a polished, metallic surface, which acts as a reflector, is worst of all in these respects. Even a surface of finely divided soot, however, does not completely absorb all the radiations which fall upon it, but exhibits a small degree of reflection. An "absolute black surface," if such could be found, would be totally devoid of reflecting power, and would absorb all the radiant energy incident upon it; and conversely would radiate all energy reaching it from its under side, without reflecting any back, or allowing any to pass through in the manner that light waves are transmitted through a transparent substance. No such perfect surface is known; but, as Kirchoff showed, it is possible to make a radiating arrangement which will give the same numerical result for the energy radiated as would be obtained by a perfect surface at the same temperature. Such an arrangement is termed a "black body," and radiations from it are designated "black-body radiations."

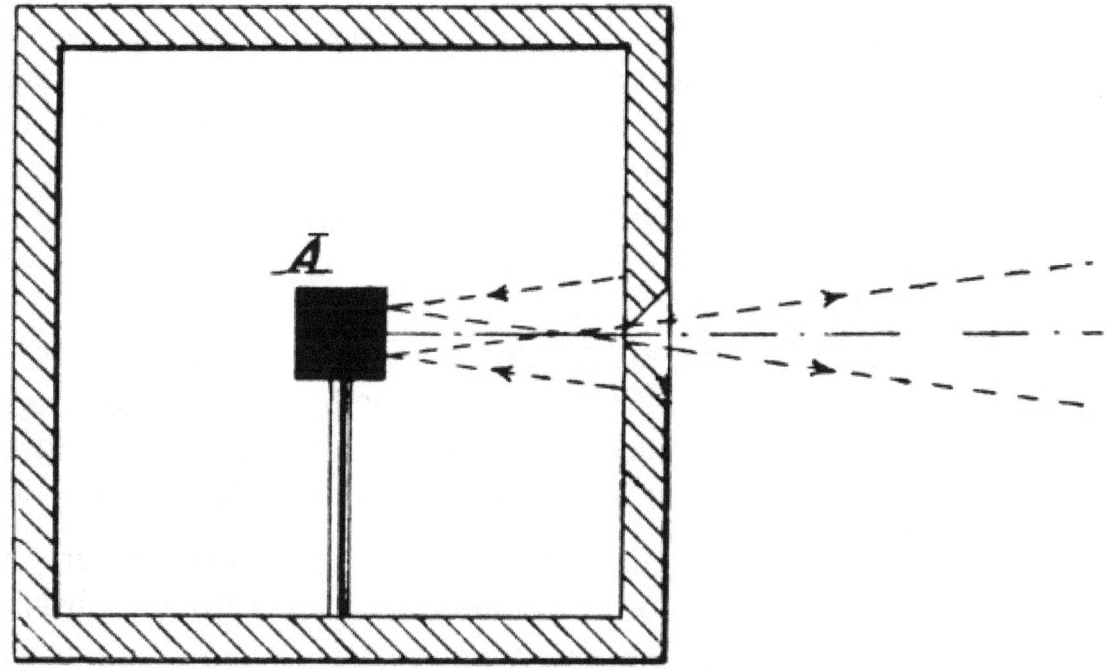

FIG. 42.—BLACK-BODY RADIATIONS.

Any enclosure, if opaque to radiant energy, and kept at a constant temperature, constitutes a black body, and radiations received from the interior through a small opening in the side are black-body radiations. Fig. 42 represents such an enclosure; in which, to show the application to pyrometry, a body A is indicated opposite to an opening in the side, through which radiations escape from the surface of A. If this surface were "perfect," all the waves falling upon it would be completely absorbed and completely radiated; but to prevent change of temperature the energy radiated must balance the energy received. If, on the other hand, the surface of A were a polished metal, the waves falling upon it from the sides of the enclosure would in the main be reflected; but here again the energy leaving the surface must equal the amount received if the temperature be constant. It follows, therefore, that if no alteration in temperature occur, the energy leaving the surface of A is independent of the nature of that surface; and the amount escaping through the opening will therefore be the same, whatever be the character of the surface opposite the opening. With a good radiating surface the rays from the enclosure will first be absorbed and then radiated through the opening; in the case of a poor radiating surface, the rays will be directly reflected through the opening; the total energy escaping being the same in either case. It will be seen later that radiation pyrometers are based upon black-body radiations; and it is important to note that the arrangement under discussion is realised in a furnace at a constant temperature, in which A might represent an object such as a block of steel. It happens, therefore, that the condition of perfect radiation is attained by the appliances in everyday use; and, moreover, black-body radiations can always be secured by placing a tube, closed at one end, in the heated space, and receiving the radiations through the open end; for this again represents an enclosure at a constant temperature. Similarly, radiations from a solid in the interior of the tube of the electric furnace shown in fig. 29 will be of the same description, and we can therefore apply with accuracy any instrument based upon black-body radiations, knowing that the same may be readily realised in practice.

The law connecting the energy radiated by a substance, under given conditions, with its temperature, was variously stated by different observers until Stefan, in 1879, deduced the true relation from certain experimental data obtained by Tyndall. Stefan concluded that the figures given by Tyndall indicated that the energy radiated by a given solid varied as the fourth power of its absolute temperature. Numerous experiments, under different conditions, showed that the fourth-power law did not apply to all kinds of surfaces or circumstances; but a strong confirmation of its truth when applied to black-body radiations was forthcoming in 1884, when Boltzmann showed, from thermodynamic considerations, that the quantity of energy radiated in a given time from a perfect radiator must vary as the fourth power of its absolute thermodynamic temperature. Certain assumptions made by Boltzmann in this investigation were subsequently justified by experiment; and numerous tests under black-body conditions have since amply verified the law. It is upon the Stefan-Boltzmann law that radiation pyrometers are based; the energy received by radiation from the heated substance, under black-body conditions, being measured by the instrument, and translated into corresponding temperatures on its scale.

Expressed in symbols, the fourth-power law takes the form—

$$E = K(T_1^4 - T_2^4),$$

where E is the total energy radiated; T_1 the absolute temperature of the black body; T_2 the absolute temperature of the receiving substance, and K a constant depending upon the units chosen. If E be expressed as watts per square centimetre, the value of K is $5 \cdot 6 \times 10^{-12}$; if in calories per square centimetre per second, the value is $1 \cdot 34 \times 10^{-12}$. The introduction of the temperature of the receiving substance, T_2, is rendered necessary by the fact, previously cited, that energy will be radiated back to the hot body, and the net loss of energy will evidently be the difference between that which leaves it and that which returns to it from the receiving substance. If T_2 were absolute zero, the energy leaving the black body would be $K(T_1)^4$; whereas if T_2 were equal to T_1, the loss of energy would be nil, as a substance cannot cool by radiation to a lower temperature than its surroundings. The temperatures T_1 and T_2 refer to the thermodynamic scale (page 9), but as the gas scale is practically identical, Centigrade degrees may be used, measured from absolute zero, or -273°. An example is appended to illustrate the application of the law:—

> *Example.*—To compare the energy radiated through an opening in the side of a furnace at temperatures of 527°, 727°, and 927° C. respectively, to surroundings at 27° C.
>
> The quantities will be as

$$K(800^4 - 300^4) : K(1000^4 - 300^4) : K(1200^4 - 300^4).$$

since 273 must be added to each temperature to convert into absolute degrees. Dividing each by K, and expanding in each case, the ratio becomes

$$(4096 - 81) \times 10^8 : (10000 - 81) \times 10^8 : (20736 - 81) \times 10^8.$$

Dividing each by 10^8 and subtracting, the result is

$$4015 : 9919 : 20655, \text{ or } 1 : 2\cdot47 : 5\cdot12.$$

It will be noted in the above example that the effect of the surrounding temperature, taken as 27° C., is small in quantity, and becomes proportionately less as the temperature of the furnace increases. If T_2 had been ignored in the calculation, the amounts of energy radiated would have appeared as

$$1 : 2\cdot44 : 5\cdot06.$$

It will be seen later, that in calculating the temperature scale of a radiation pyrometer, the temperature of the surroundings is for this reason not taken into account. Fig. 43 is a graphic illustration of the fourth-power law.

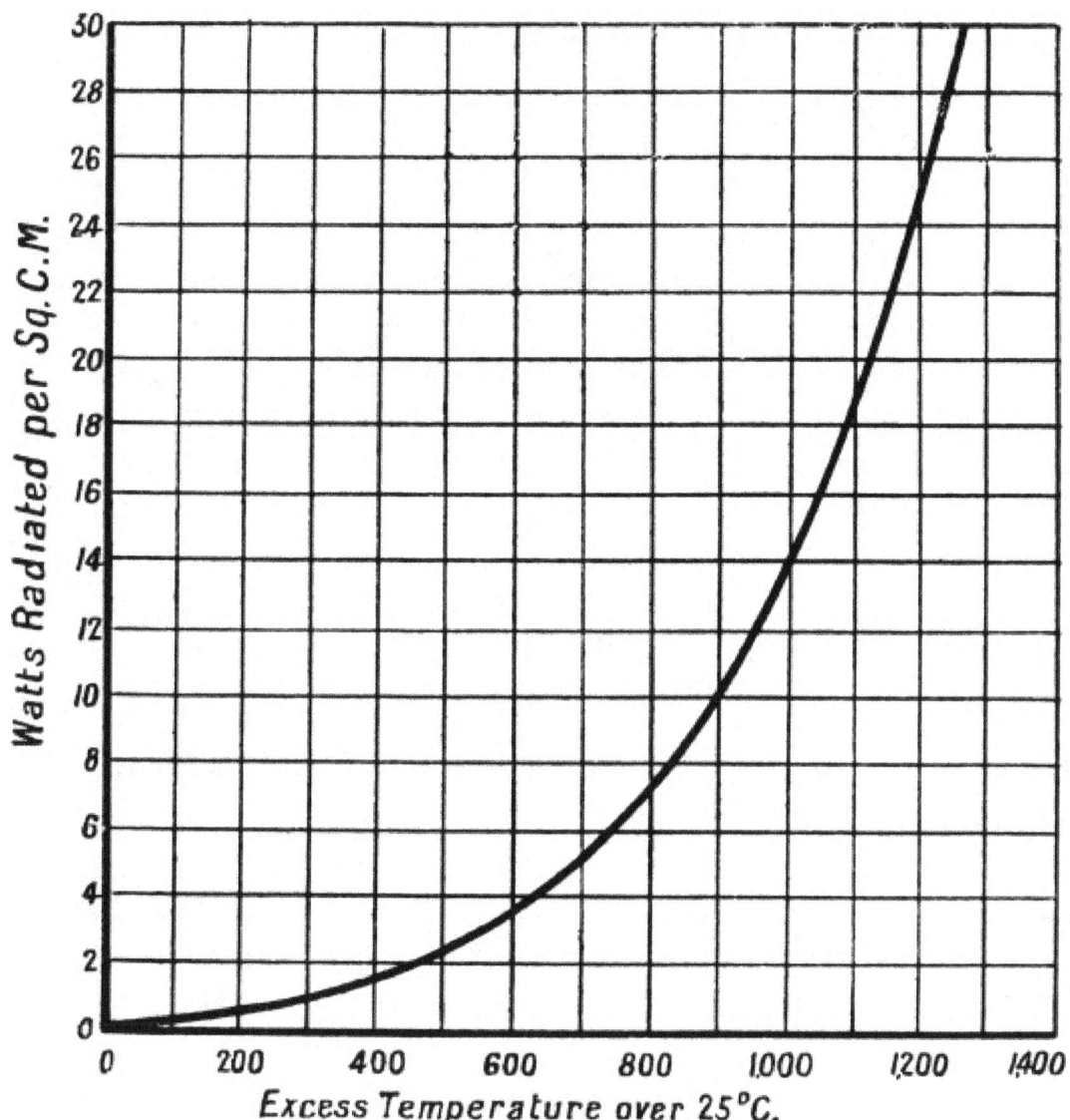

FIG. 43.—ENERGY RADIATED BY A BLACK BODY AT DIFFERENT TEMPERATURES.

When the relation between temperature and quantity of energy radiated is known, any instrument which will indicate the amount of the radiations it receives may be used to measure temperatures. The ray, for example, may be focused on a thermal junction, which will be heated in proportion to the amount of energy incident upon it, and when connected to a millivoltmeter will cause deflections proportional to the energy it receives. A thin strip of metal might be used in place of a junction, and by measuring its resistance the heating effect of the radiations, and hence the amount thereof, may be deduced. A third method would be to focus the rays on to a compound strip of two metals, which by altering in shape could be made to furnish a clue to the quantity of energy received by it. In theory, it is only necessary to allow the radiations to fall on the working part of any instrument for measuring low temperatures, when the rise in temperature produced may be taken as proportional to the energy received, and the thermal condition of the radiating body deduced from the fourth-power law. In practice, however, it is desirable that the receiving thermometer should be small in size; of low thermal capacity, so as to respond rapidly; and capable of giving a sensitive indication—hence an ordinary mercury thermometer would be unsuitable for this purpose. A thermopile, placed at a fixed distance, would fail owing to the cold junctions gradually warming up by conduction through the pile. The part receiving the radiations should be coated with lamp-black, so that practically all the waves impinging upon it, whether luminous or non-luminous, may be absorbed, and the energy they represent utilised in producing a rise in temperature.

Practical Forms of Radiation Pyrometers: Féry's Instruments.— In the year 1902 Féry introduced a pyrometer in which the rays were focused by the aid of a lens upon a small, blackened thermal junction, in the same way that the rays of the sun may be focused by a burning-lens. The junction was connected to a special form of d'Arsonval galvanometer, which recorded the E.M.F. developed. By taking the readings of the galvanometer as proportional to the temperature of the junction—that is, to the radiant energy impinging upon it—the temperature of the source could be calculated from the fourth-power law. The drawback to the use of this instrument was the fact that a proportion of the rays was absorbed by the glass, this proportion, moreover, varying at different temperatures, so that the fourth-power law could not be applied with accuracy. By using a fluorspar lens in place of glass, this error was overcome, but the cost of a good lens of this material being high, its use in ordinary workshop practice was rendered prohibitive on account of the price. A number of these pyrometers, furnished with glass lenses, and calibrated by comparison with a standard possessing a fluorspar lens, were placed on the market, but were superseded in 1904, when Féry hit upon the plan of focusing the rays by means of a concave mirror, thus overcoming the error due to absorption by the glass lens. This plan, which serves admirably, has since been adopted in most radiation pyrometers.

Féry's Mirror Pyrometer.—This instrument is shown in longitudinal and also in cross section in fig. 44. A concave mirror, M, which has a gilt reflecting surface, is placed at one end of a metal tube, and is fastened to a rack which engages in a pinion moved by the milled-head, P, so that on turning P, a longitudinal movement is imparted to the mirror. A small, blackened thermal junction, shown at the centre of the cross section, and consisting of a copper disc to which wires of copper or iron and constantan are fastened, receives the rays after reflection, and may be brought into focus by suitably moving the mirror.

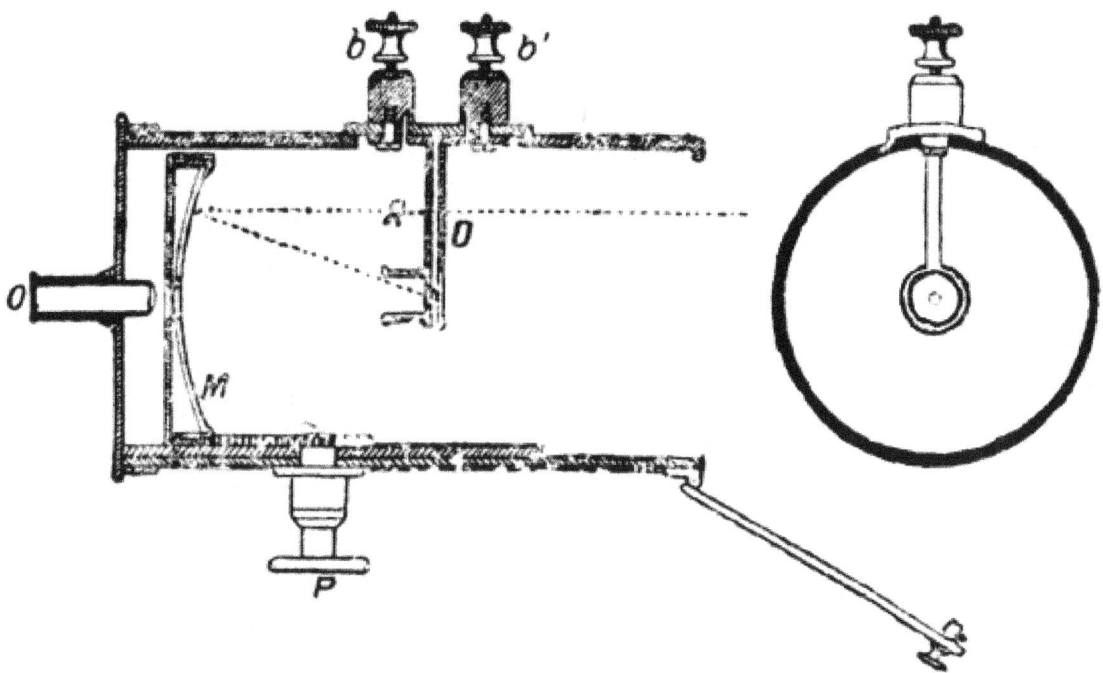

FIG. 44.—FÉRY'S MIRROR PYROMETER. SECTION.

Fig. 45.—Féry's Mirror Pyrometer. End View.

The wires pass to terminals b and b′ on the outside of the tube, from which leads are taken to the indicator. In order to discover when the junction is in the focus of the mirror, an eye-piece, O, is fitted in the end of the tube, which enables the junction to be seen, magnified, through a hole in the centre of M. By means of an optical device placed near the junction, the image of the sighted object, produced by M, is reflected in two portions to the eye-piece O. When the junction is exactly in the focus of M, a circular image is seen round the junction; when out of focus, the appearance presented is that of two semi-circles not coinciding laterally. The adjustment consists in moving the mirror until the separate semi-circles produce a continuous circle; a method at once simple and definite. The front end of the pyrometer is shown in fig. 45, in which it will be seen that the entrance may be partially closed by a diaphragm, or left entirely open, as required. The diaphragm is used to cut off a definite proportion of the radiations, and is used for very high temperatures, at which, with full aperture, the indicator needle would be urged beyond the limits of the scale. On the indicator two separate temperature scales are provided, one referring to full, and the other to partial aperture. The same end might be achieved by inserting a suitable resistance in series with the indicator: but in this case the junction might be unduly heated, and possibly damaged thereby. The proportions of the pyrometer are such that at the highest temperatures measured the heat incident on the junction never raises it above 110° C. Although the intensity of radiations diminishes as the square of the distance, the quantity impinging on the junction is, within limits, independent of the distance: This arises from the property of concave mirrors with respect to the relation between the size of an image and the distance of the object producing it. If r = the radius of the mirror, u the distance of the object, and v the distance of the image, both measured from the centre of the mirror, the relation $1/u + 1/v = 2/r$ holds for a concave mirror, and when two of these are known the third may be calculated. Further, if d be the linear dimension of an object, and d_1 that of its image, the relation $d/d_1 = u/v$ also holds, and from these two expressions all the points arising in connection with the Féry pyrometer may be determined, as will best be made clear by examples.

Example I.—To find the position of the image of an object formed by a mirror of 6 inches radius, with object at distance (*a*) 10 feet, (b) 20 feet.

Reducing to inches, and applying in the formula

$$1/u + 1/v = 2/r, \quad 1/120 + 1/v = 1/3$$

and

$$1/240 + 1/v = 1/3$$

from which the values of v are $3\text{-}1/13$ inches and $3\text{-}1/26$ inches respectively, a difference of only $1/26$ of an inch.

If u were 6 inches, v would also be 6 inches; if u were infinity, v would be 3 inches. The movement of the image, when an object is brought towards it from a great distance, would in the mirror under notice be from 3 inches away to 6 inches away, and at distances of 10 feet and upwards would only differ in position by small fractions of an inch.

Example II.—To find the area of the image of a circular opening, 1 foot in diameter, formed by a mirror of 6 inches radius distant from the opening (*a*) 10 feet; (*b*) 20 feet.

Since $d/d_1 = u/v$;

then from the results of Example I,

$12/d_1 = 120/(3-1/13)$ at 10 feet distance, and

$12/d_1 = 240/(3-1/26)$ at 20 feet.

Hence the linear dimensions, *i.e.* the diameters of the circular images, will be 0·308 and 0·152 inch respectively; and the areas 0·074 and 0·0182 square inch. These areas are to each other practically as 4 : 1.

That is, the area of the image decreases in size directly as the *square* of the distance of the object; the squares of the distances being 100 and 400, or as 1 : 4; whereas the areas of the images are as 4 : 1.

Example III.—To find, for a 6-inch mirror, and a junction of $1/10$th of an inch in diameter, the greatest distance at which the mirror may be placed from an opening 1 foot in diameter, so as to give an image not less than the junction.

From Example I it is evident that at any distance exceeding 20 feet the position of the image will only be a minute and negligible fraction over 3 inches; hence v may be taken as 3.

Applying values in the formula $d/d_1 = u/v$; and taking d_1 as equal to the diameter of the junction, $= 0\cdot 1$ inch,

$12/0\cdot 1 = u/3$, and $u = 360$ inches, or 30 feet.

Beyond this distance the image would be less than the junction. The conclusions to be drawn from the foregoing examples are: (1) that the amount of energy received by the junction does not vary, provided the image overlaps it; and (2) that the limiting distance at which a correct reading can be secured is that at which the size of the image is equal to that of the junction. Thus, taking distances of 10 and 20 feet, as in Example II; at the former distance the energy striking the mirror is four times as great as with the latter; but, on the other hand, the area of the image at 10 feet distance is four times as great as that obtained at 20 feet. Hence, at the greater distance, the proportion of the image impinging on the junction is four times as great, and the fact that only ¼ the amount of energy strikes the mirror is thus counterbalanced. All the reflected rays which fail to strike the junction are ineffective, and pass out through the entrance of the tube.

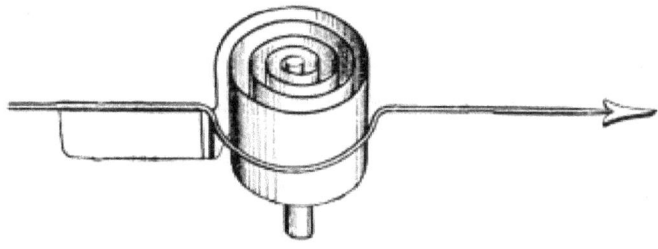

FIG. 46.—FÉRY'S SPIRAL.

The two-scale form of instrument described above is extremely useful for general purposes, but when all the temperatures to be controlled fall within the limit of one of the scales, it is simpler and cheaper to dispense with the diaphragm, and to use an indicator furnished with one scale only. The single-scale mirror pyrometer is for this reason more generally employed for industrial purposes; and the Cambridge and Paul Instrument Company now make a pivoted indicator for use with full aperture, which is less liable to damage than one which possesses a suspended coil.

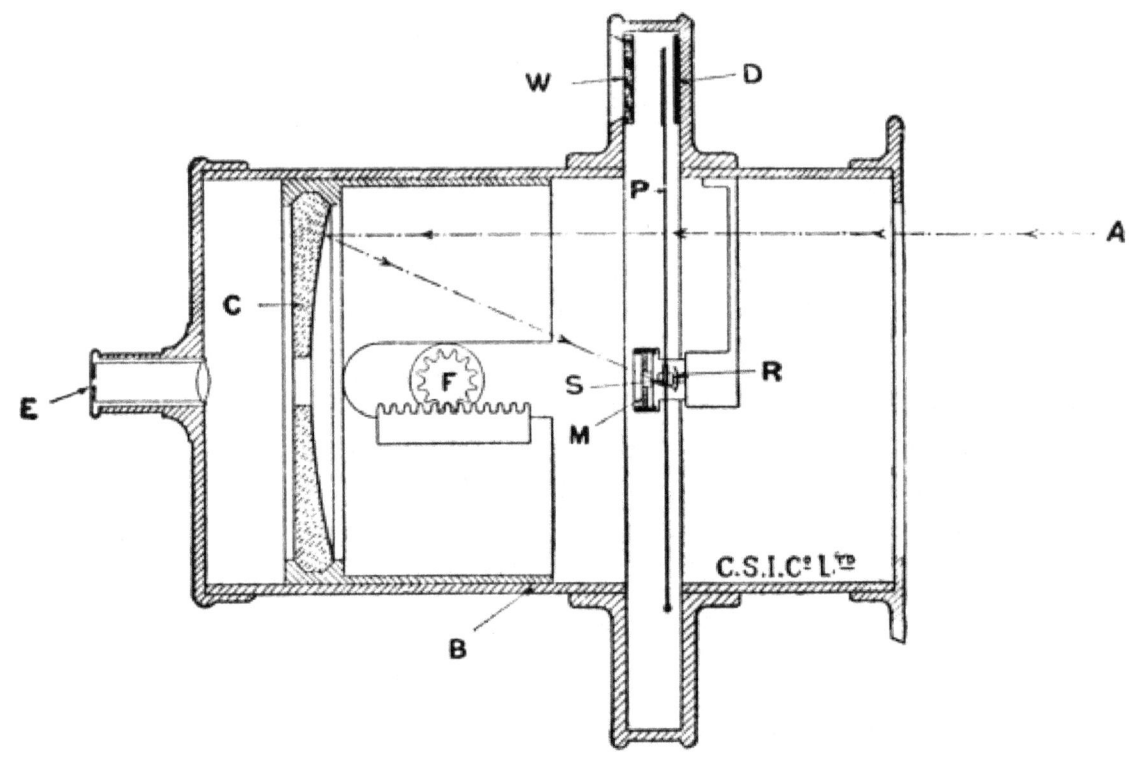

FIG. 47.—FÉRY'S SPIRAL PYROMETER. SECTION.

Féry's "Spiral" Radiation Pyrometer.—This instrument differs from the preceding merely in the fact that the rays are focused on a small spiral, formed of a compound strip of two metals, fixed at one end and furnished with a pointer at the free-moving end (fig. 46). The effect of alterations of temperature on this spiral are to cause it to coil up or uncoil, according to whether the temperature rises or falls. This movement is magnified by the pointer, the end of which moves over a dial graduated to read temperatures directly. This arrangement is shown in section in fig. 47, where C is the mirror, E the eye-piece, S the spiral, P the pointer, and D the dial, viewed through the window W. The appearance of the apparatus when viewed from the front is shown in fig. 48. The advantage gained by the use of the spiral is that the instrument is self-contained, no galvanometer being necessary; but, on the other hand, the indications are not so exact, an error of 20° C. being probable at temperatures over 1000° C. In using this pyrometer, it is observed that after focusing the hot substance, the pointer moves rapidly for a time and then pauses, after which it again commences to creep along the scale. The temperature indicated at the moment the pause occurs is generally taken as the reading, but this is not always correct.

FIG. 48.—FÉRY'S SPIRAL PYROMETER. FRONT VIEW.

The creeping movement is probably due to the whole instrument, and the air in the interior, becoming heated by the entering rays, and by proximity to the hot source. In a number of trials made by the author, it was noticed that when the instrument was allowed to stand near the furnace for some time before using, thereby attaining the temperature existing in the vicinity, the "creep" almost entirely vanished. All things considered, the spiral form of Féry's pyrometer must be regarded as more portable but less accurate than that in which the rays are received on a thermal junction.

Foster's Fixed-Focus Radiation Pyrometer.—The necessity for focusing, common to all Féry's radiation pyrometers, is obviated in Foster's pyrometer, which, however, cannot be used from so great a distance. The principle involved in the fixed-focus pyrometer is that the amount of energy received by a concave mirror and focused on a thermal junction will not vary so long as the area of the surface sending rays to the mirror, through a fixed opening, increases as the square of the distance. This will be understood from fig. 49, in which C is the mirror, D a thermal junction fixed so as to be in the focus of the opening E F, and A B the heated surface. The lines joining E and F to the edge of the mirror intersect in a point G, and provided the lines G E and G F, if produced, fall within the heated surface A B, the quantity of energy falling on D will always be the same. A cross section of the cone G A B is a circle; and if A B be twice as far away from G as E F, the areas of the circles of which A B and E F are diameters will be in the ratio 4: 1. But as A B is twice as far from G as E F, the intensity of its radiations will be as 1: 4; and hence loss of radiating power is exactly balanced by increase in area.

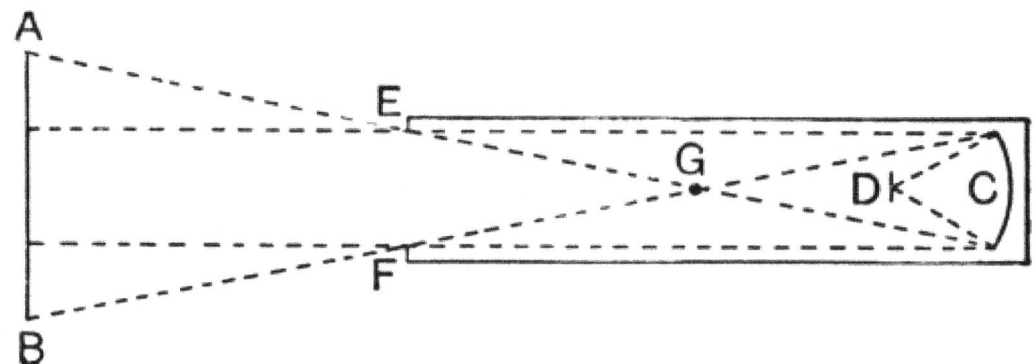

FIG. 49.—PRINCIPLE OF FOSTER'S FIXED-FOCUS PYROMETER.

In the actual instrument the tube in which the mirror is placed is blackened internally, so that no rays reach the mirror by reflection from it. The diameters of the opening E F and the mirror C are such that the perpendicular from G on to A B is ten times the length of A B. Hence, if the heated object be 6 inches in diameter, the limiting distance of G is 10 × 6 = 60 inches. The position of the point G is indicated by a ring on the outside of the tube, and in taking a measurement the tube is brought well within the distance prescribed, which is in all cases ten times the diameter of the heated object. Temperatures are read from a galvanometer connected to the thermal junction, the whole arrangement being portable, as shown in figs. 50 and 51, which represent the instrument in use.

FIG. 50.—FOSTER'S PYROMETER, MOUNTED ON STAND.

The advantages derived from the use of a fixed focus instrument are simplicity and cheapness; but, as many occasions arise in practice in which focusing on an object is a necessity, Foster's pyrometer must be regarded as a simplified apparatus not capable of the wider applications of Féry's instruments, but of great service in many cases. Whipple has recently adapted the Féry spiral pyrometer to produce an instrument with a fixed focus, by fastening the instrument to a fireclay tube, on the closed end of which the pyrometer is permanently focused. This form is specially useful for determining the temperature of molten metals, into which the end of the fireclay tube is plunged, thus giving true black-body conditions.

FIG. 51.—FOSTER'S PYROMETER, IN USE.

Paul's Radiation Pyrometer.—Thwing, in America, has introduced a radiation pyrometer in which the rays from the furnace enter the wide end of a cone, and by internal reflection are brought to the apex, at which a thermal junction is located. Paul, in this country, has marketed a similar instrument, the action of which is shown in fig. 52, where E is a tube containing a polished cone, C, at the apex of which is fixed a thermal junction, T. Rays from the hot source A A´ enter the tube at D, and pass into the cone, being finally reflected on to T, which is connected to the indicator. So long as the lines joining the outside of the cone with the extremities of the entrance D, crossing at O, fall within the hot source, A A´, the reading will be the same at all distances. Fig. 53 shows the actual pyrometer, mounted on a tripod.

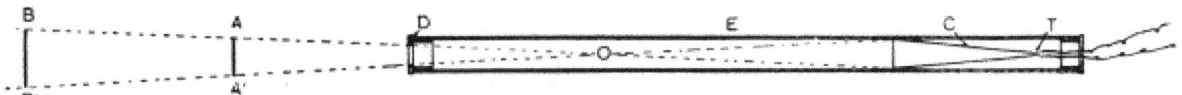

FIG. 52.—PRINCIPLE OF PAUL'S RADIATION PYROMETER.

Indicators for Radiation Pyrometers.—When the radiations are focused on a thermal junction, the temperature of which is raised in consequence, the E.M.F. developed is in accordance with the laws discussed in Chapter II, and any thermo-electric indicator, if sufficiently sensitive, will serve for the purposes of a radiation pyrometer. The effect on the galvanometer is influenced by: (1) the nature of the junction; (2) the size of the mirror or cone; and (3) the highest temperature attained by the junction. The indicators used in connection with radiation pyrometers are of the pivoted type, which can now be made sufficiently sensitive to give full-scale deflection for a rise of 100° C. in the temperature of the junction. For the junction itself, Heil's alloy (zinc and antimony in atomic proportions) partnered with constantan has been used, owing to the high E.M.F. developed; but cases of deterioration of this alloy have been noted, causing it to be replaced by some makers by iron. Two iron or copper constantan junctions in series give an E.M.F. for a rise of 100° C., sufficient to work a pivoted indicator, and are preferable to Heil's couple for a radiation pyrometer.

Fig. 53.—Paul's Radiation Pyrometer.

Calibration of Indicators for Radiation Pyrometers.—The deflections on the indicators are due to the E.M.F. generated, which is proportional to the difference in temperature between the hot and cold junctions. If both these are at the same temperature—say, 20° C.—the deflection is zero; and on allowing the radiations to fall on the hot junction its temperature is raised by an amount depending upon the intensity of the radiations—say, to 90° C. The deflection produced is then due to a difference of (90 - 20) = 70°, the radiations having raised the temperature of the hot junction 70° above its surroundings. If the surroundings (including the cold junction or junctions) had been at 15° to commence with, the hot junction under the same conditions would have risen to 85°, giving again a difference of 70°, and thus causing the same deflection as before. Provided both hot and cold junctions are located so as to attain the same atmospheric temperature in the absence of radiations, a given quantity of energy impinging on the hot junction will always produce in it the same *excess* temperature, and will therefore give rise to the same deflection at all ordinary atmospheric temperatures. As the junctions are so arranged in radiation pyrometers as to fulfill this condition, no correction for fluctuations in the cold junctions is necessary. The deflections, therefore, correspond to excess temperatures of the hot junction, which in turn are directly proportional to the energy received by the junction. Readings in millivolts on the indicator thus represent directly the proportions of energy received by the hot junction, 4 millivolts corresponding to twice the energy, which produces 2 millivolts, and so on; and hence the millivolt scale becomes an energy scale.

In order to translate energy into corresponding temperatures, the fourth-power law must be applied. If E_1 correspond to an absolute temperature T_1 on the part of the black body from which radiations are received, and E_2 correspond to another temperature T_2, the following relations will hold good:

$$E_1 = K(T_1^4 - x^4), \quad \text{and} \quad E_2 = K(T_2^4 - x^4),$$

where x is the temperature of the surroundings receiving the radiations. As previously pointed out (see Example on page 140), the term x^4 may be ignored for the range of high temperatures measured by a radiation pyrometer, hence $E_1 = K T_1^4$, and $E_2 = K T_2^4$; and therefore $E_1 / E_2 = T_1^4 / T_2^4$. But, as shown above, readings in millivolts on the indicator are directly proportional to the energy received, and if R_1 and R_2 = millivolts due to E_1 and E_2, the relation $R_1/R_2 = T_1^4/T_2^4$ is then obtained.

In order to prepare a temperature scale from this relation, it is necessary to take one correct reading at a known temperature, after which the remainder of the scale may be marked by calculation, as shown in the example appended:—

Example.—A tube closed at one end is at 927° C. (1200° abs.), and gives a deflection corresponding to 2 millivolts on the indicator. To find the temperatures which would yield deflections due to 1, 3, 4, and 5 millivolts.

Taking the case of 1 millivolt and applying in the formula

$$R_1/R_2 = T_1^4/T_2^4 \quad ; \quad 2/1 = 1200^4/T_2^4$$

from which $T_2^4 = 1200^4/2$ and $T_2 = 1009°$ abs. = 736° C. Similarly, 3 millivolts represent 1055° C.; 4 millivolts = 1154° C.; and 5 millivolts = 1236° C. These values are readily obtained by the use of four-figure logarithms.

Having calculated the temperature corresponding to each whole millivolt, a curve may be plotted to represent millivolts against corresponding temperatures, and intermediate values deduced from it. Evidently, the standard reading must be taken with great accuracy, as the whole scale hinges upon it; and for this purpose an accurate resistance or thermo-electric pyrometer may be used, placed inside the tube of an electric furnace, and the radiation pyrometer sighted on a thin sheet of iron placed just in front of the naked junction. A check at the higher readings of the scale is necessary, as an exact realisation of the fourth-power law is seldom obtained in practice. This may be taken in the same manner, as thermocouples may now be calibrated directly against the gas scale up to 1550° C., thus enabling the gas-scale reading to be transferred to the radiation pyrometer. For delicate readings over a given range, the scale of a mirror galvanometer may be calibrated in this manner, sufficient resistance having first been added in series to ensure that at the highest temperature employed the spot of light will remain on the scale.

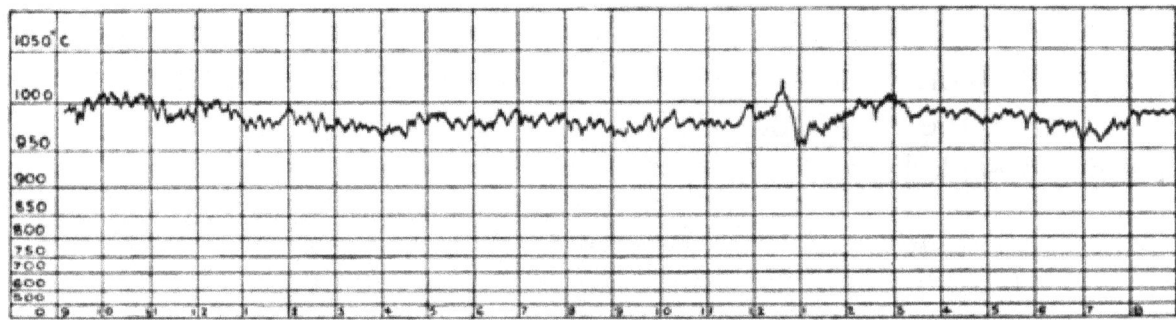

Fig. 54.—Record obtained with Radiation Pyrometer.

Recorders for Radiation Pyrometers.—Any of the thermo-electric recorders described in Chapter II may be applied to radiation pyrometers, the chart being suitably divided according to the fourth-power law. When taking a record, the pyrometer is fixed on a stand or bracket and focused on the desired spot. Fig. 54 is an example of a record taken with a Thread recorder and Féry pyrometer, in which the division of the temperature scale according to the fourth-power law will be noticed. It is possible to arrange that the working temperature shall lie on the open part of the scale, by adjusting the sensitiveness of the galvanometer accordingly before calibrating.

Management of Radiation Pyrometers.—It is not advisable to place a radiation pyrometer in the hands of an unskilled observer, as intelligent oversight is required if good results are to be secured. Care must be taken to adjust the galvanometer needle to zero before taking a reading, and the needle should always be locked during transit. When focusing on an object in a furnace it is necessary to make certain that the red image seen is actually that of the object, which may be done by moving the pyrometer until the side of the object, or some special feature, is visible in the eye-piece, when the pyrometer may be moved until the image surrounds the junction. Occasions may arise, as in taking the temperatures of various zones of a rotary cement-kiln or other furnace, in which it is required to focus the mirror for a specified distance; in which case the author has adopted the plan of placing a fixed pointer opposite the milled head which controls the mirror (P, fig. 44) and focusing the bars of a window at measured distances, marking the same on the milled head opposite the pointer; and it would be a convenience if all radiation pyrometers were thus marked initially. A good check to correct focusing in the case of a heated object is to alter the focus in both directions, and finally to adjust to the maximum reading, which should correspond to the true focus.

Great care should be taken not to damage the mirror. If, in a workshop, the surface become covered with dirt, this should be removed by gentle brushing with a camel-hair brush or by blowing air over the mirror. The focusing device should never be strained beyond its working limits; when these are reached, the pyrometer should be moved bodily until the object can be correctly sighted within the ordinary limits of the movement of the milled head. If metallic fumes or dense smoke intervene between the furnace and the pyrometer, the radiations will be impeded and the temperature recorded will be too low; and in such cases the pyrometer should be placed at the open end of a tube and sighted upon the closed end, which should terminate at the spot under observation.

In all cases it must be borne in mind that the indications only apply to black-body conditions. If a block of steel be sighted inside a furnace, and then be removed to the exterior and again sighted, the external reading will be much less than the internal, owing to the inferior radiating power of the surface, which now derives no assistance from the furnace. All readings should therefore be taken whilst the object is still in the furnace, or (as in taking the temperature of molten metal in a ladle) a fireclay tube with a closed end inserted in the mass may be used, and readings taken through the open end. Statements are sometimes made that the difference between external readings and black-body readings is constant for a given surface, and that the one may be translated into the other; but this is true only for unchanging surfaces, such as platinum, and seldom applies to ordinary working surfaces. As black-body conditions are so easy to ensure, it is simpler and safer always to arrange to take observations under such conditions, rather than to trust a relation seldom constant in practice.

When using a radiation pyrometer for a number of furnaces, fireclay tubes, closed at one end, may be inserted in each, so that the closed end terminates at the working spot, the open end being left flush with the exterior of the furnace. The diameter of such tubes will depend upon the length and also upon the make of the pyrometer; in all cases the image of the closed end must be large enough to overlap the receiving junction or spiral. Information on this point can always be obtained from the makers, or can be discovered by trial with openings of known diameter. When using the pyrometer to obtain temperatures in the interior of the tube of an electric furnace, such as that illustrated in fig. 29, a solid object, such as a short fireclay cylinder, or a piece of graphite, should be placed in the middle of the tube, and focused on the junction.

Special Uses of Radiation Pyrometers.—For regular use at temperatures above 1000° C. or 1850° F. the radiation pyrometer will be found to be more useful than instruments of the thermo-electric or resistance type as the latter undergo deterioration owing to the continuous action of the furnace gases, which becomes more marked as the temperature increases. Examples of industrial processes in which 1000° C. is considerably exceeded are the manufacture of glass, pottery, and cement, the treatment of special steels, and the casting of metals and alloys. Even for temperatures between 750° and 1000° C. a radiation pyrometer may be used, but is not so convenient for this range as a thermo-electric instrument. There is no upper limit to the instrument, which may be calibrated by the fourth-power law to the highest temperature attainable, that of the electric arc, which has been found to be 3720° C. by the use of a Féry radiation pyrometer. Measurements may therefore be made beyond the limits of thermal junctions, such as the temperature of electric furnaces and of thermit in the mould, and of molten steel before pouring, thus opening out the possibility of accurate control at extremely high temperatures. There is always a danger, however, of the cold junction becoming unduly heated when near to large masses at very high temperatures, and serious errors may arise from this cause. Two examples may be cited to illustrate the usefulness of the radiation pyrometer in practice: (1) the hardening of steel projectiles; and (2) the determination of the temperature of the clinkering zone in a rotary cement kiln. In (1) the projectile is brought to a given spot near the brink of the furnace, where it is in the focus of a radiation pyrometer, and when at the specified temperature is raked out of the furnace and drops into an oil-trough. It has been found that a difference of 10° C. from the standard temperature at which the projectiles should be quenched may cause a serious lowering of the penetrative power of the finished projectile; and hence a radiation pyrometer, which may readily be sighted on each individual shell, is the best to use for this purpose. In (2) the hottest spot may be found by focusing the pyrometer to different distances up the kiln, and, by taking a record, any fall in temperature due to defect of coal or air supplies, or to excessive feed of raw material, may be detected, thus furnishing information from which the process may be regulated to the best advantage. At the temperatures prevailing in such kilns—1300° to 1450° C., or 2370° to 2640° F., according to the nature of the kiln—a Féry radiation pyrometer is quite sensitive to changes of 10° C. or 18° F., and the author has found it to be entirely satisfactory in this connection. The adaptability of radiation pyrometers to all temperatures above a red heat, combined with the absence of deterioration, renders these instruments of great value, and the possibility of obtaining records is a further recommendation. The radiation method, however, is not suited to the purposes of an installation, as even if mirrors and junctions could be constructed so as to be identical, the arrangement would be very costly. A cheap adaptation of the radiation principle, by means of which a number of furnaces, such as a set of cement-kilns, could be controlled from a centre, would be of great advantage, and would add further to the general utility of this class of pyrometer.

CHAPTER VI
OPTICAL PYROMETERS

General Principles.—When a solid is heated to 450° C., it commences to send out luminous radiations and appears a dull-red colour in a darkened room. As the temperature rises, the luminous radiations become more intense; the colour changes to a lighter red, then to orange, yellow, white, and finally to a dazzling white. Attempts have been made to assign temperatures to specified colours, and Pouillet, in 1836, introduced a table which purported to give the relation between colour and temperature. The following table, published by Howe in 1900, differs considerably from that of Pouillet, who had no accurate means of measuring the temperatures he assigned to the colours:—

Description.	Temp. Deg. C.	Temp. Deg. F
Lowest red visible in darkness	470	878
” ” ” daylight	475	887
Dull red	550 to 625	1022 to 1157
Full cherry	700	1292
Light red	850	1562
Full yellow	950 to 1000	1742 to 1832
Light yellow	1050	1922
White	1150	2108

If it were possible for all observers to detect exactly the colours to which these temperatures refer, the table would be of great utility; but in practice any two persons might differ in judgment to the extent of 50° C. below a yellow; and when the white is reached, and becomes dazzling, accurate discrimination is impossible. At the same time, a trained workman, used to quenching steel at a fixed temperature, say 850° C., acquires a high degree of judgment with constant practice, and may not vary by more than 20° C. at temperatures below a light yellow. The personal equation, however, is too great for colour judgment by the unaided eye to be taken as an accurate guide to temperature. A fairly close approximation, however, may be obtained by matching the colours against prepared standards, as will be referred to later.

The determination of the intrinsic brightness of the heated substance by a photometric method naturally suggests itself as a possible means of ascertaining temperatures by optical means, and it will be found that all the optical pyrometers used for industrial purposes are based on this procedure. The law connecting the intensity of the whole of the light waves emitted with temperature, for a given solid, is approximately given by Rasch's formula:—

$$\frac{I_1}{I_2} = \left[\frac{T_1}{T_2}\right]^x$$

where I_1 and I_2 are the intensities corresponding to absolute temperatures T_1 and T_2; and the exponent

$$x = \frac{25000}{T_1}$$

Hence at 1250° abs. the brightness increases as the 20th power, and at 2500° abs. as the 10th power of the temperature. This rapid increase in brightness for a small rise in temperature enables small increments to be readily observed; but a difficulty arises in practice owing to vast differences in brightness displayed by different substances at the same temperature. For example, the light emitted by an incandescent gas-mantle, which consists of thorium oxide, is vastly greater than that given out by a metal, such as platinum, at the same temperature; and it is therefore evident that the luminosity of a substance depends not merely upon its temperature, but also upon its nature. It is possible, however, to obtain indications for any substance in terms of a black body; thus if a heated solid possessed the same intrinsic brightness as a black body at a temperature of T, the "apparent" or "black-body" temperature of the solid would also be called T. All that this would signify would be that the condition of the solid was such that the light radiated was equal in intensity to that emitted by a black body at temperature T; and to obtain the true temperature of the solid, T must be multiplied by a factor which expresses the ratio of its emissive power to that of a black body.

In all photometric methods a standard light is employed, which should not vary in brightness, and with which the light from the source is compared. In optical pyrometers no attempt is made to measure the illumination in terms of candle-power; all that is necessary is to bring the standard and the source to the same degree of brightness by suitable adjustments. Amongst the standards employed are carbon-filament electric lamps, amyl-acetate lamps, and for higher temperatures the centre of an acetylene gas-flame; each of which is capable of producing a fixed degree of brightness when used under specified conditions. A black body, at known temperatures, is compared with the standard used, thus furnishing a scale of "black-body" temperatures to which the indications of a given source may be referred, as explained in the previous paragraph. Above 1000° C., however, the light becomes too dazzling to enable a proper comparison of the standard and source to be made, and absorbing glasses must then be used to reduce the brightness. Any coloured glass, taken at random, might not reduce the standard and source equally; but if a monochromatic glass be used—that is, a glass which transmits light of one wave-length only—a well-defined relation is found to exist between the intensity of the transmitted light and the temperature of the source. As optical pyrometers are used for temperatures above 1000° C. in most cases, involving the use of such glass, it will be necessary briefly to consider the relations between the wave-lengths of light and the temperature of the radiating substance, which in all cases will be assumed to be a black body.

Wien's Law.—When the temperature of a substance increases, the enhanced brightness which results is shared by all parts of its spectrum; and if the substance were viewed through a glass prism, it would be noticed that every portion was brighter than before. Taking a ray of wave-length λ, the relation between its intensity and the temperature of the (black-body) source is given by Wien's formula:—

$$J = c_1\lambda^{-5} \times e^{-(c_2/\lambda T)} \qquad (1)$$

where J = energy corresponding to wave-length λ; e = the base of the natural system of logarithms; T = absolute (thermodynamic) temperature of the black-body source, and c_1 and c_2 are constants, the values of which may be found by measuring J at two known temperatures for light of a known wave-length. Experiment has shown that this formula is correct for wave-lengths which lie in the visible spectrum, but does not hold for longer waves; and modifications of Wien's equation have been given by Planck and others which are of more extended application. For the purposes of optical pyrometry, however, using red light of wave-length about 65 millionths of a centimetre, Wien's law may be applied with great accuracy; and a calibration based upon this law agrees closely with the values obtained by other pyrometric methods.

Wien's formula may be written in the form—

$$\log_{10} J = K_1 + K_2 (1/T) \qquad (2)$$

where $K_1 = (\log c_1) - (5 \log \lambda)$ and $K_2 = c_2(\log e/\lambda)$. This simplified expression shows a linear relation between log J and $1/T$; and hence if the temperatures corresponding to two intensities be known, the results may be plotted on squared paper in the form of a straight line connecting T and J, from which line intermediate or extraneous readings of temperatures may be obtained for any given intensity. Another useful form of Wien's equation, referring to the ratio of two intensities J_1 and J_2, is as under:—

$$\log(J_1/J_2) = \frac{c_2 \log e}{\lambda}(1/T_2 - 1/T_1) \qquad (3)$$

where T_2 and T_1 are the absolute temperatures corresponding to J_2 and J_1 The value of c_2 is 1450000, when λ is expressed in millionths of a centimetre. Evidently, if the ratio J_1 / J_2 and the value of c_2, λ, and T_2 be known, T_1 may be calculated. When λ is not known, as in the case of a piece of red glass for which its value has not been determined, two readings at known temperatures will establish the value of $(c_2 \log e) / \lambda$, all the other results may then be calculated. Examples illustrating the application of the formula will now be given.

Example I.—A black body at an absolute temperature T_1 is found to give twice the intensity observed at 1200° abs., the comparison being made with red glass transmitting wavelength 65×10^{-6} cms. To find the value of T_1.

Applying values to formula (3)

$$\log 2 = (1450000/65) \log 2 \cdot 7183 \times (1/1200 - 1/T_1)$$

and

$$0 \cdot 3010 = (1450000 \times 0 \cdot 4343/65) \times (1/1200 - T_1/1)$$

from which $T_1 = 1237°$ abs.

Example II.—The intensity of the radiations from a black body at 2000° abs. are found to be equal to those from a given standard, taken as unity. To find the intensity at 3000 abs., compared with the same standard. $\lambda = 65 \times 10^{-6}$ cms.

Applying in (3) as before,

$$\log(J_1/1) = (1450000 \times 0 \cdot 43435/65) \times (1/2000 - 1/3000)$$

from which $\log J_1 = 1 \cdot 615$, and $J_1 = 14 \cdot 5$.

In applying Wien's law to the calibration of an instrument in which the intensity of a source may be measured photometrically against that of a standard, an electric furnace (fig. 29) may be used, with a piece of iron in the centre, coated with oxide, which gives black-body radiations. A thermo-electric pyrometer in contact with the oxide may be used to measure the standard temperatures, and brightnesses may then be compared with that of an amyl-acetate or other lamp giving a flame of constant luminosity. Temperatures corresponding to other intensities may then be deduced by calculation, as previously shown.

Practical Forms of Optical Pyrometers.—The instruments used in practice fall under the following heads:—

1. The standard light is constant, and the intensity of the light from the source varied in the instrument until equal to the standard. (Féry, Le Chatelier, Wanner, and Cambridge.)

2. The standard is varied until equal to that of the source, which may be reduced in intensity if this exceed that of the standard. (Holborn-Kurlbaum, made in commercial form by Siemens.)

3. The colour of the source is matched against a standard colour, made to agree with that obtained in a given operation (Lovibond); or the source may be made to produce a standard colour by a polarising device (Mesuré and Nouel); or the colour of the source is extinguished by suitable absorbents (various forms).

Examples of each type will now be described.

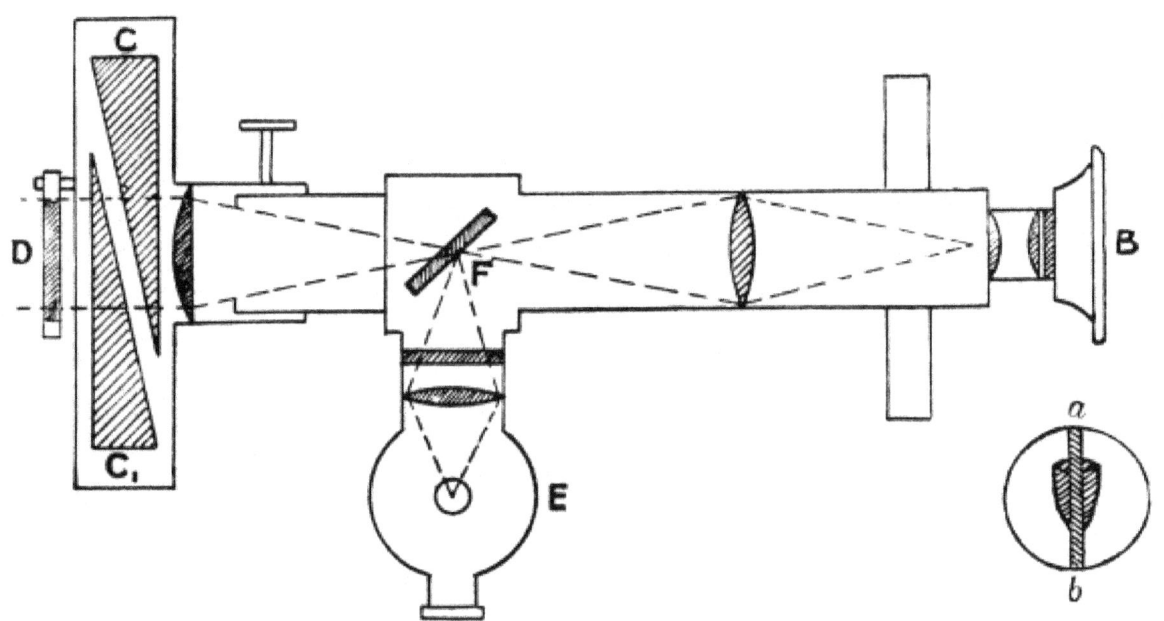

Fig. 55.—Féry's Optical Pyrometer. Section.

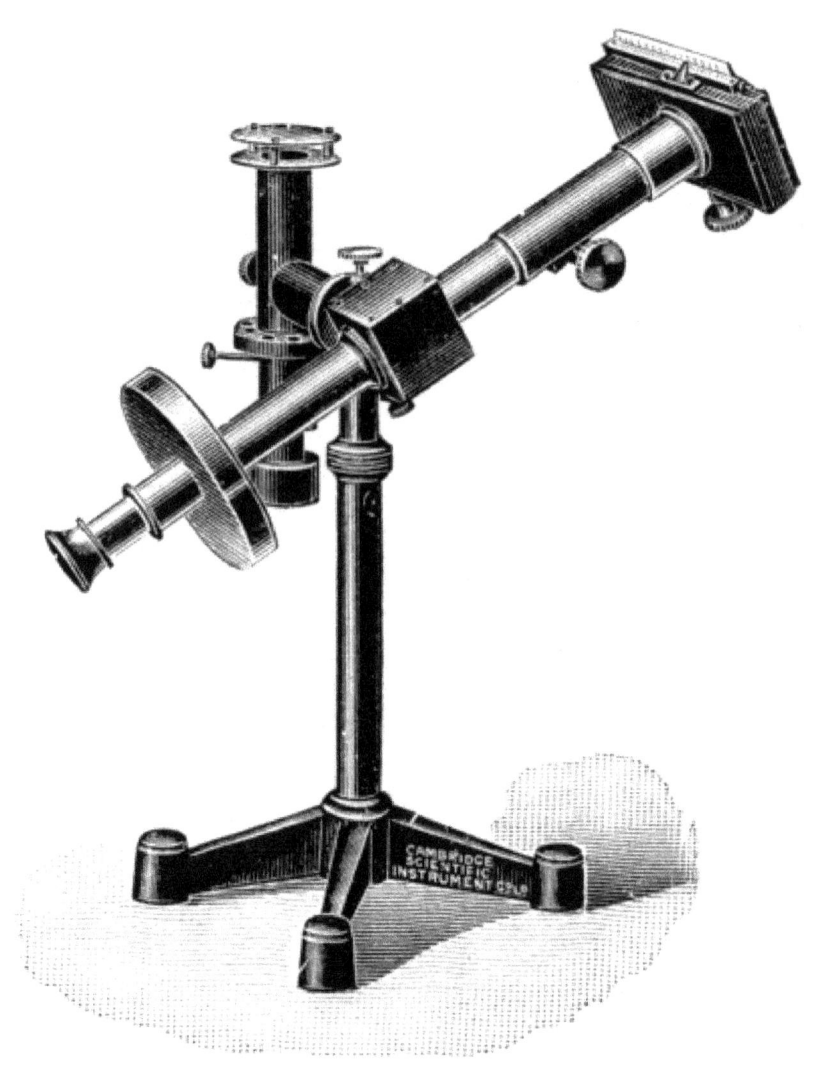

Fig. 56.—Féry's Optical Pyrometer. External View.

Féry's Optical Pyrometer.—This instrument (shown in figs. 55 and 56) consists of a telescope furnished with a side-branch, in which a standard lamp E is placed. Light from E is focused upon a piece of transparent glass F, inclined at an angle of 45° to the axis of the telescope, from whence it is reflected into the eye-piece. To render the light received from the lamp monochromatic, a piece of red glass is interposed between E and the mirror. The telescope is sighted on the hot substance, rays from which pass through a piece of red glass D, and thence through two wedges of darkened glass, which diminish the intensity to a greater or less degree according to the thickness of absorbent glass interposed, which is reduced by sliding the wedges apart, and increased by the contrary movement. After passing through the wedges, the light proceeds through the inclined mirror to the eye-piece; consequently, the appearance presented to the eye is that of a field illuminated one-half by the standard lamp, and the other by the hot source. The adjustment consists in sliding the wedges, by a screw movement, until both portions of the field are equally illuminated. A temperature scale is provided on the moving piece which actuates the wedges, and is derived by Wien's equation from the thickness of the wedges interposed when equality is obtained. Calibration is effected by noting the thickness of the wedges corresponding to two known temperatures, from which a straight line connecting thickness with the reciprocal of the absolute temperatures may be drawn, and a table formed giving values of T in terms of the thickness of the wedges. The calibration may be extended indefinitely, the accuracy of the readings depending upon the truth of Wien's law. Féry's optical pyrometer is a convenient instrument for occasional readings of high temperatures, combining simplicity with portability.

Le Chatelier's Optical Pyrometer.—This pyrometer was the original form of instrument in which the temperature of a luminous source was deduced by photometric comparison with a standard light; and Féry's apparatus, described above, is merely a convenient modification of the original. Instead of the absorbent glass wedges, Le Chatelier employed an iris diaphragm to reduce the quantity of light entering the telescope; the adjustment being carried out by altering the size of the opening in the diaphragm until the brightness of the source agreed with that of the standard. The intensity of the light received in the telescope will vary as the square of the diameter of the opening; and calibration at two known temperatures with a given monochromatic glass enables a temperature scale corresponding to diameter of opening to be computed by Wien's law. Le Chatelier's pyrometer is a valuable implement for research work in the laboratory, but is not so convenient for workshop purposes as Féry's modification.

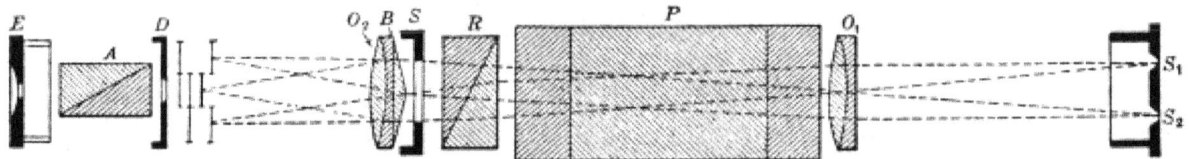

Fig. 57.—Wanner's Pyrometer. Section.

Wanner's Pyrometer.—The principle of this pyrometer is the comparison of the brightness of a red ray from the standard with that of the ray of some wave-length obtained from the source, both rays being produced spectroscopically and therefore being truly monochromatic. The brightness is compared by the aid of a polarising device, resulting in a somewhat complicated optical arrangement, which is shown in fig. 57. Light from a standard electric lamp passes through the slit S_1, and from the hot source through S_2. Both beams are rendered parallel by means of an achromatic lens O_1, which is placed at a distance equal to its focal length from the slits. The parallel beams are dispersed by the direct-vision spectroscope P; and then pass through the polarising prism R, which separates each beam into two beams, polarised in planes at right angles. A biprism, B, placed in contact with a second achromatic lens, O_2, is made of such an angle that two fields of red light, polarised in planes at right angles, one from the source and the other from the standard, are focused on the slit D. These fields are viewed through an analyser A, and are brought to equal brightness by rotating the analyser, to which a graduated scale is attached, the temperature being deduced from the angle through which the analyser is turned. The calibration is effected by Wien's law (equation (3) page 172), the intensities of standard and source being related to the angle of rotation as indicated by the equation. $J_2/J_1 = \tan^2 \Theta$ where J_2 and J_1 represent the intensities of source and standard respectively, and Θ = angle of rotation. Introducing this value into Wien's equation (page 172), the relation between Θ and T may be shown to take the form $\log \tan \Theta = a + b/T$, where a and b are constants. Hence, if $\log \tan \Theta$ be plotted against $1/T$ a straight line is obtained, and hence by a few observations at known temperatures a calibration curve may be drawn from which intermediate and extraneous readings may be obtained. Messrs Hadfield have introduced a special chart, divided so that actual readings in degrees C. may be taken directly by observing the angle Θ. As sent out for use, the temperature scale is prepared beforehand, so that direct readings may be taken.

As the standard electric lamp will vary in brightness with repeated use, means must be provided to restore it to its proper value. This can be done by placing a rheostat in the circuit of the lamp, and adjusting the current until the brightness, as viewed through the pyrometer, exactly agrees with that of a ground-glass surface illuminated by a standard amyl-acetate lamp. The flame of this lamp really constitutes the standard; but as it would be blown about by air-currents when used in a workshop, the electric lamp, lighted by a portable battery, is brought to equality and used for general measurements.

Cambridge Optical Pyrometer.—During the recent war the manufacture of pyrometers of this type was taken up by the Cambridge and Paul Instrument Company. The external form of the Cambridge optical pyrometer is shown in fig. 58, in which an observer is shown using the instrument, the accessories consisting of a 4-volt accumulator, an ammeter, and an adjustable resistance for regulating the current through the electric lamp used for comparison; and a standard amyl-acetate lamp for adjusting the electric lamp to the correct brightness. The scale is marked on a circular disc, and direct readings are obtained from the position of a pointer which rotates with the analyser. By interposing a monochromatic glass to dim the source, the range of the pyrometer can be modified; and instruments are provided in four ranges: 700°—1400° C.; 900°—2000° C.; 1200°—2500° C., and 1400°—4000° C.

The Cambridge optical pyrometer has proved a useful instrument in skilled hands, and has been found of great service in the steel, glass, and pottery industries. Trained observers have found it possible to detect a difference of 10° C. at the region of 1900° C. The adjustment of the two fields to equality, however, involves a judgment which varies with different observers, and in practice it is advisable for one individual to be entrusted to take all readings.

Fig. 58.—Cambridge Optical Pyrometer.

Holborn-Kurlbaum Pyrometer.—In the optical pyrometers previously described a constant standard is used, and the brightness of the light from the source varied until equality is obtained. The idea of varying the brightness of the filament of an electric lamp until its colour matched that of the source, and deducing the temperature from the current taken by the lamp, was due to Morse, who used a filament in the form of a flat spiral, heated by a battery of E.M.F. 40 volts. This spiral was placed in a metal tube and interposed between the eye and the heated object. The Holborn-Kurlbaum pyrometer, as made by Siemens, is a refinement of that of Morse, and capable of reading over a more extended range. In fig. 59, L is a small electric lamp with a hairpin filament, as shown at A. This lamp is placed in a telescope, so that the filament is in the focus of the eye-piece and is lighted by a 4-volt accumulator, in series with which is a rheostat, R, and a milliammeter, M. The heated source is focused by moving the object-glass of the telescope, and both lamp and source are viewed through red glass placed in front of the eye-piece, D. The rheostat, R, is then adjusted until the tip of the filament is indistinguishable from the background, which is illuminated by the source. If the lamp be too bright, the filament will appear as a bright line; if duller than the source, as a dark line; and when equal to the source it will merge into the background. When equality is obtained, the milliammeter is read, and the temperature deduced from the current taken by the lamp.

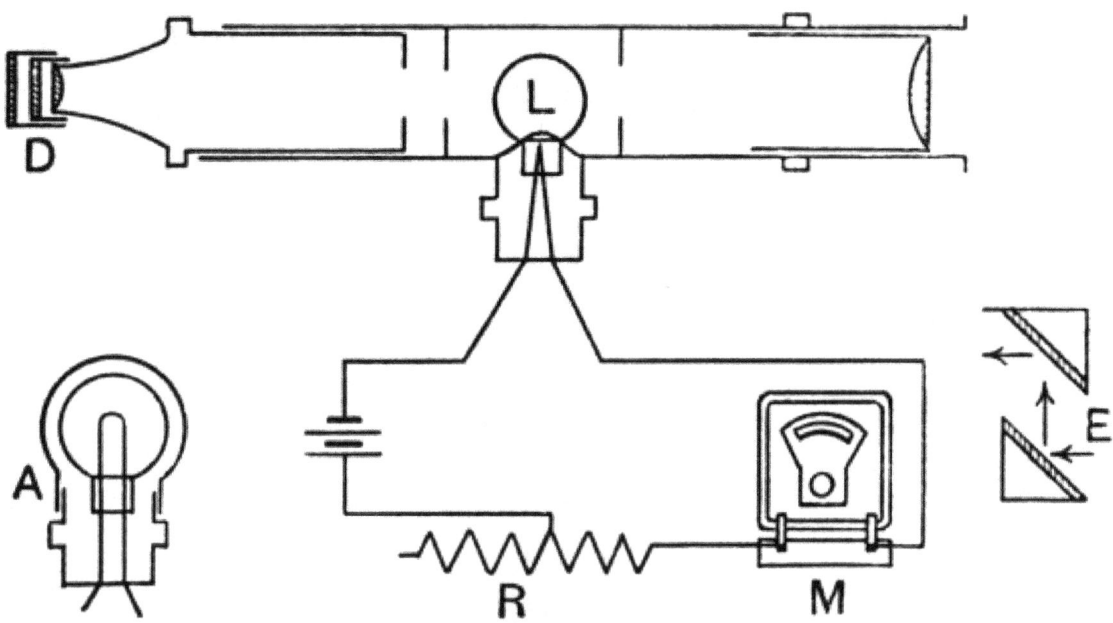

FIG. 59.—HOLBORN-KURLBAUM PYROMETER. SECTION.

The relation between current and the temperature of the filament varies with each lamp, but is in all cases represented by a formula of the type

$$C = a + bt + ct^2$$

where C = current, t = temperature in degrees C., and a, b, and c are constants depending upon the lamp used, and which can be determined by making a number of observations at known temperatures. The instrument is calibrated in this manner by the makers, and a scale affixed from which temperatures may be read corresponding to observed currents.

When the temperature of the source exceeds that of the standard at maximum current, an absorbing device, E, consisting of two prisms of darkened glass, with their reflecting faces parallel, is placed over the end of the telescope, so as to reduce the intensity of the source below that of the lamp. A separate calibration is performed with the absorber in position, and a second temperature scale provided, from which readings are taken when the absorbing device is used. Fig. 60 represents the instrument as made by Messrs Siemens, for use in a fixed position, the telescope, milliammeter, and rheostat being mounted on an upright supported by a tripod, and the current obtained from a portable accumulator. A second form (fig. 61) is designed for use in cases when observations at a number of different places are required, the rheostat being mounted on the telescope, and the milliammeter contained in a leather case provided with shoulder-straps.

FIG. 60.—SIEMENS' OPTICAL PYROMETER, ON STAND.

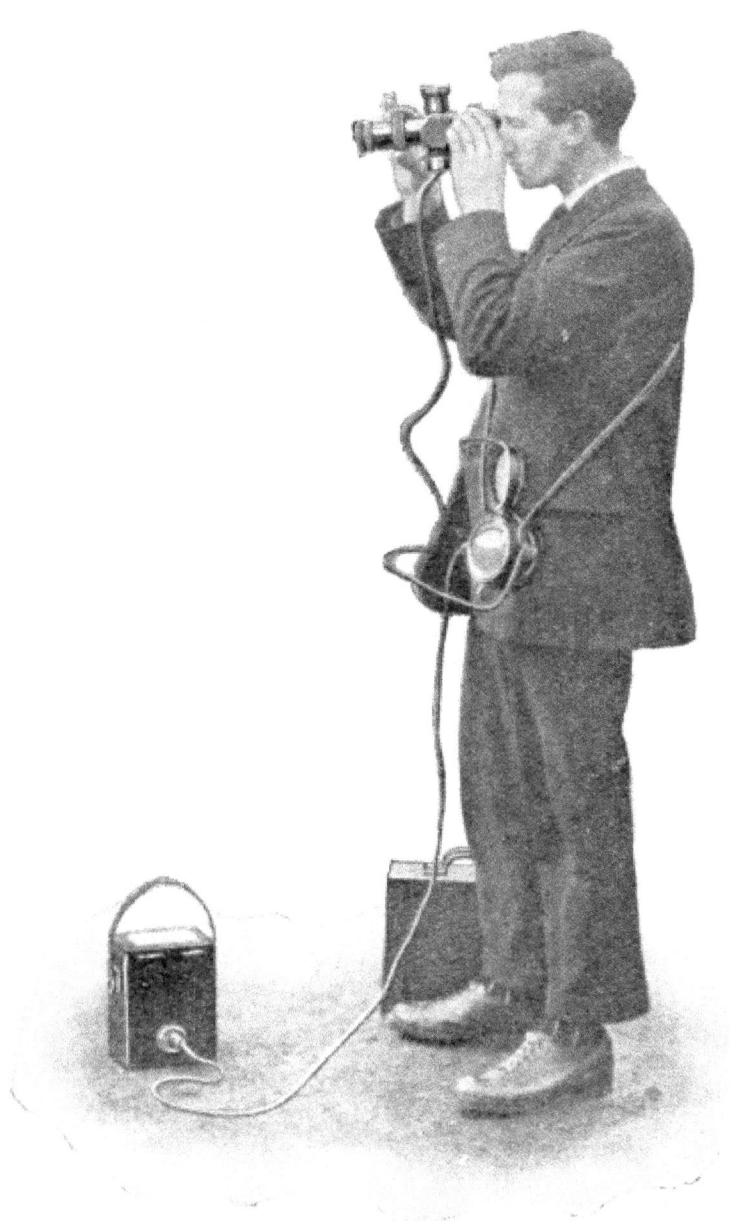

FIG. 61.—SIEMENS' OPTICAL PYROMETER, PORTABLE FORM.

The adjustment in this pyrometer is simple, and the condition of equality sharply defined. Whereas, in matching the colours of two contiguous fields, separate observers may disagree to an extent representing 40° C. or more, a divergence of 10° C. is seldom exceeded when different operators adjust the tip of the filament to extinction. In a special test to decide this point, the author compared the observations of five persons, some trained and others untrained, with the result that all agreed to within 10° at a steady temperature in the vicinity of 1200° C.; and in this respect the Holborn-Kurlbaum pyrometer is superior to other forms of optical pyrometer. The continuous accuracy of the readings depends upon the permanence of the standard lamp, which is ensured by over-burning for 20 hours, after which the lamp may be used at its proper voltage for a long period without further change. As used for occasional readings in the workshop, such a lamp will last for a year or more without varying in brightness by an amount representing 10° C. at a temperature of 1800° C. When a new lamp is used, a fresh calibration is necessary; the makers, however, in such case send out a new temperature scale with the lamp.

Lovibond's Pyrometer.—It is possible, by the use of coloured glasses superposed, to match closely any given colour; and Lovibond, whose tintometer for this purpose is well known, has applied this method to temperature measurement. Taking the case of a block of steel in a furnace, it is possible to arrange combinations of glasses which, when illuminated by a standard light, will give the same tint as the steel at any specified temperature. If it be desired to work the steel at 850° C., for example, glasses are provided which, when viewed by the light transmitted from a 4-volt glow-lamp, using a constant current, represent the tint of steel at 840°, 850°, and 860° respectively. The image of the steel is reflected by a mirror through one hole in a brass plate, which forms the end of a wooden box, at the opposite end of which an eye-piece is placed. A second hole in the brass plate receives light from the standard lamp, after passing through the glasses; and the appearances of the two lights are then compared. A skilled eye can readily detect a disagreement in the two fields corresponding to 10° C.; and by introducing the glasses in turn it can be observed whether the steel is within 10° C. of the temperature required. This instrument is cheap and simple, but is obviously only useful in deciding a pre-arranged temperature, as to take a measurement at an undefined temperature would involve an unwieldy number of glasses, and absorb a considerable time. The correct glasses to use for a given operation are decided under working conditions at temperatures measured by a standard pyrometer; after which any number of instruments may be made from glasses of the same colour and absorptive power as those used in the calibration. Correct matching is difficult below 700° C.

Mesuré and Nouel's Pyrometer.—This instrument, shown in [fig. 62](), consists of two Nicol prisms, between which is placed a piece of quartz cut perpendicularly to its axis. Light from the source, in passing through the first Nicol prism, is all polarised in the same plane; but on passing through the quartz is polarised in various planes, according to the wave-length. The colour seen after passing through the second prism, used as analyser, will depend upon the angle between this and the first or polarising prism. The analyser is connected to a rotating disc, divided into angular degrees; and on viewing the heated source the colour will appear red if the analyser be turned in one direction, and green if rotated in the opposite. The intermediate colour is a lemon-yellow; and the adjustment consists in rotating the analyser until this tint is obtained. The angular reading is then taken, and the temperature read off from a table prepared by making observations at known temperatures. Observers may disagree by as much as 100° C. in using this pyrometer, owing to differences in eyesight and judgment of the lemon-yellow tint; but a given operator, who has trained himself to the use of the instrument, may obtain much closer results with practice. The chief use of this device is to enable a judgment to be formed as to whether a furnace is above or below an assigned temperature, within limits of 25° C. on either side at the best; and hence it is convenient for a foreman or metallurgist to carry about for this purpose when other pyrometers are not in use. A great advantage is that the instrument is always ready for use, and has no accessories.

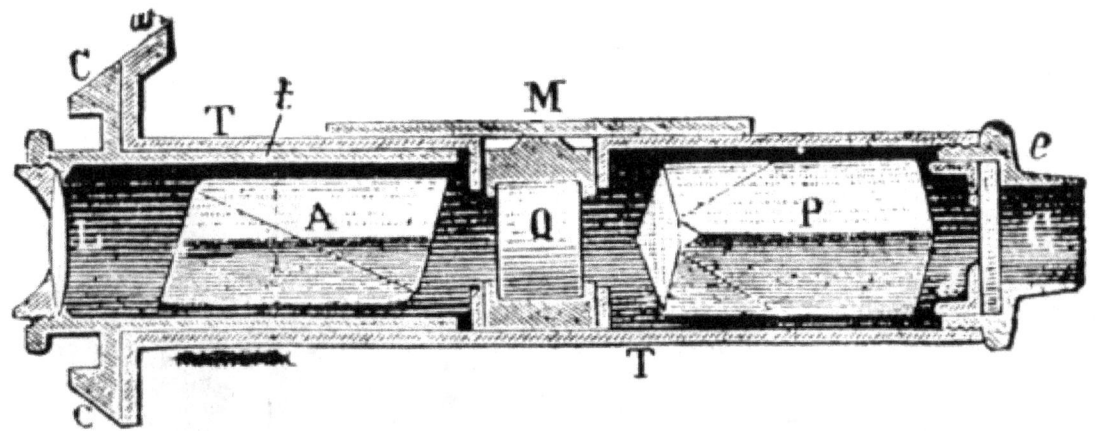

FIG. 62.—MESURÉ AND NOUEL'S PYROMETER.

Colour-extinction Pyrometers.—Various attempts have been made to produce superposed glasses, or cells of coloured fluids, which will have the effect of extinguishing the colour of a heated source. As an example, three cells containing various dyes in solution may be prepared which, when looked through, will extinguish the colour at 840°, 850°, and 860° C. respectively. If it be desired to work at 850°, a difference of 10° on either side may be detected by a trained eye; but to follow a changing temperature a large number of cells would evidently be necessary. Heathcote's extinction pyrometer, in its early form, consisted of an eye-shade in front of which two pairs of cells containing coloured fluid were mounted. In bringing a furnace to an assigned temperature, observation was made from time to time until a faint red image was perceived through one pair of cells, when the heat supply was regulated so as to maintain the existing temperature. When viewed through the second pair of cells, which contained a slightly darker fluid, no red image was to be seen at the correct temperature. With training, a workman could control a furnace to a fair degree of accuracy by this means, but the operation was tedious, and useful only for the attainment of a single temperature. In a later instrument, known as the "Pyromike" (fig. 63), Heathcote employs a single cell with flexible walls, so that by turning the screw-end, the length of the column of fluid interposed between the eye and the furnace can be altered. In taking a reading, the furnace is sighted and the screw turned so as to increase the length of the column of coloured fluid, until the image is no longer visible. A direct reading of the temperature is then obtained on a spiral scale marked on the cylindrical body of the instrument, over which the screwed portion rotates. This forms a simple and convenient temperature gauge for workshop use.

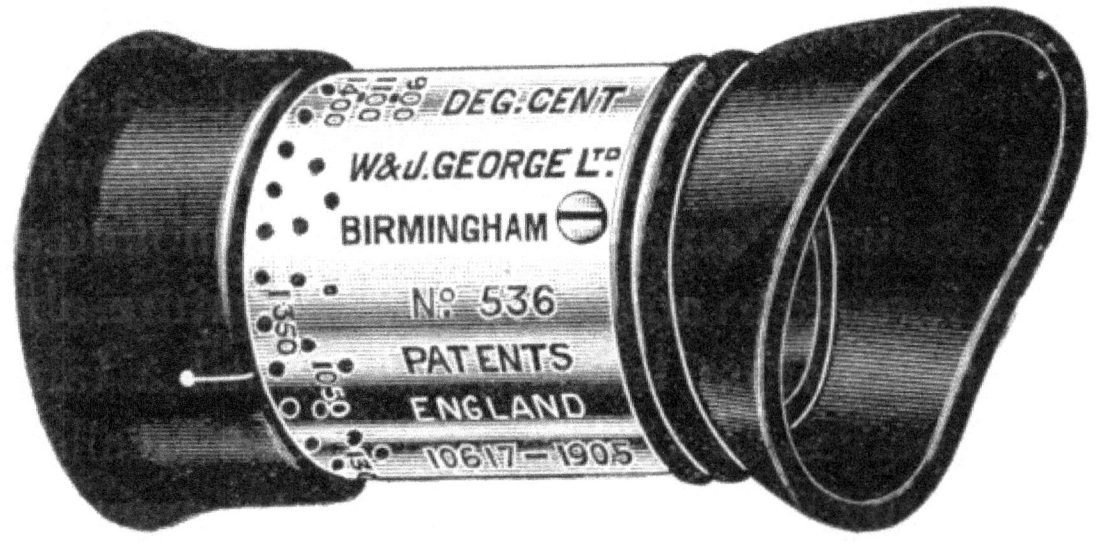

Fig. 63.—Heathcote's Extinction Pyrometer or "Pyromike."

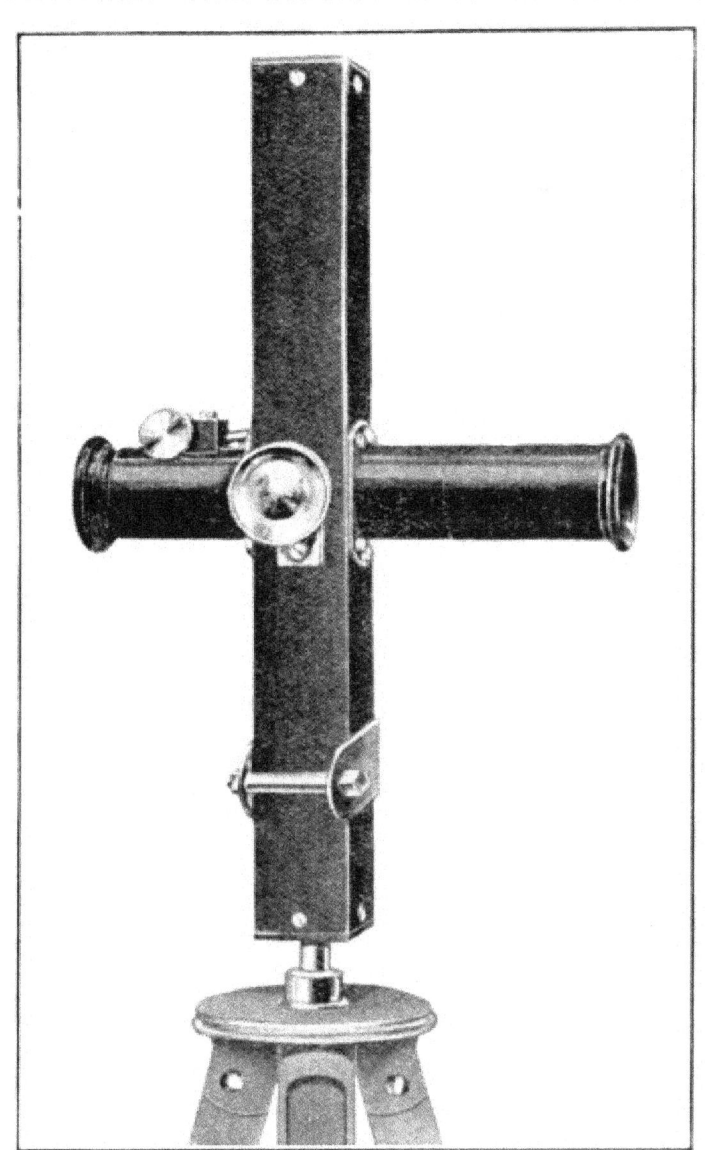

Fig. 64.—"Wedge" Pyrometer.

The "Wedge" Pyrometer, designed by Alder and Cochrane (fig. 64), consists of a small telescope through which a prism of darkened glass may be moved, and which is focused on the heated object. By turning a head the wedge may be moved so as to interpose a thicker layer of dark glass between the eye and the furnace, and the same operation causes a temperature scale to pass in front of a fixed pointer. When the image of the hot source is just extinguished, the temperature is read from the mark opposite the fixed point. Training is needed to enable an observer to judge the exact point of extinction, when it becomes possible to obtain results of 20° C. in the region of 1300° C. On the other hand, when used by one unaccustomed to the instrument, the reading may be wrong by 50° C. or more. As an aid to the judgment near the extinction point, the hand may be interposed between the telescope and furnace, when, if extinction be complete, no alteration should be observed in the field of view. The simple construction of this pyrometer is an advantage, no accessories being needed; and when used with the precautions stated above, readings sufficiently close for many processes can easily be obtained.

Management of Optical Pyrometers.—Careful usage is essential with optical pyrometers, which are liable to get out of adjustment with rough handling; and for this reason a trained observer should be in charge of such instruments. Skilled attention is equally requisite in taking readings, as the matching of tints correctly is an operation which demands a high degree of judgment. Careful attention must be paid to the standard lights; if flames, regulation to the standard height is essential; if electric lamps, care must be taken not to use them for a longer period than necessary, in order to increase the useful life. Accumulators should be recharged regularly—say once in two weeks—to keep in good order. Separate parts, such as absorption glasses, should be kept in a place of safety, as their destruction may involve a new calibration. It should be kept in mind that the temperatures indicated by optical pyrometers are "black" temperatures; that is, they correspond to the readings that would be given by a black-body of the same degree of brightness. In consequence, readings should always be taken under black-body conditions, the precautions in this respect being identical with those necessary for total-radiation pyrometers, given on page 163. In some special cases the connection between the apparent and true temperatures has been worked out for a given type of pyrometer, but, owing to the different emissive powers of different substances, no general relation can be given.

Special Uses of Optical Pyrometers.—The advantageous use of optical pyrometers is restricted to observations at temperatures beyond the scope of instruments which have the working part in the furnace; or to cases in which occasional readings of temperature suffice. To follow a changing temperature continuous adjustment is necessary, involving labour, and therefore costly. Amongst workshop uses may be mentioned: (1)

ascertaining the temperature of pottery kilns and glass and steel furnaces; (2) in the treatment of steels at very high temperatures, to which end the pyrometer may be set to a given reading, and the process carried out when the steel is observed to attain such assigned temperature; (3) to take casual readings when a number of furnaces are in use, or when a number of sighting-holes are provided, as in large brickmaking furnaces; and (4) for occasional observations of the firing end of rotary cement kilns. As an instrument of research in the laboratory, a good form of optical pyrometer is very useful, as, for example, in investigating the working temperatures of electric lamps, and taking observations in electric furnaces. It is a great drawback that records cannot be taken by optical pyrometers, as much valuable information can be gathered from an accurate knowledge of temperature fluctuations in most operations. This disadvantage must always militate against the general use of these instruments.

CHAPTER VII
CALORIMETRIC PYROMETERS

General Principles.—If a piece of hot metal, of known weight and specific heat, be dropped into a known weight of water at a temperature t_1, which rises to t_2 in consequence, the temperature of the hot metal, t_0, can be obtained by calculation, as shown by the following example:—

> *Example.*—A piece of metal weighing 100 grams, and of specific heat 0·1, is heated in a furnace and dropped into 475 grams of water, contained in a vessel which has a capacity for heat equal to 25 grams of water. The temperature of the water rises from 5° to 25° C. To find the temperature of the furnace.
>
> The heat lost by the metal is equal to that gained by the
> water and vessel. Equating these,
>
> $$100 \times 0\cdot1 \times (t_0 - 25) = (475 + 25) \times (25 - 5)$$
>
> from which $t_0 = 1025°$ C.

The above calculation, which applies generally to this method, depends for its accuracy upon a correct knowledge of the specific heat of the metal used. This value is far from constant, increasing as the temperature rises, and the result will only be correct when the average value over a given range is known.

The metal used in the experiment should not oxidise readily, and should possess a high melting point. Platinum is most suitable, but the cost of a piece sufficiently large would considerably exceed that of a thermo-electric or other outfit. Nickel is next best in these respects, and is now generally used for the calorimetric method, up to 1000° C. The specific heat varies to some extent in different specimens, but can be determined for the ranges involved in practical use. This may be done by heating a given weight to known temperatures and plunging into water, the result being obtained as in the foregoing example, t_0 in this case being known and the specific heat calculated. From a series of such determinations, a curve may be plotted connecting specific heat and temperature range, from which intermediate values may be read off.

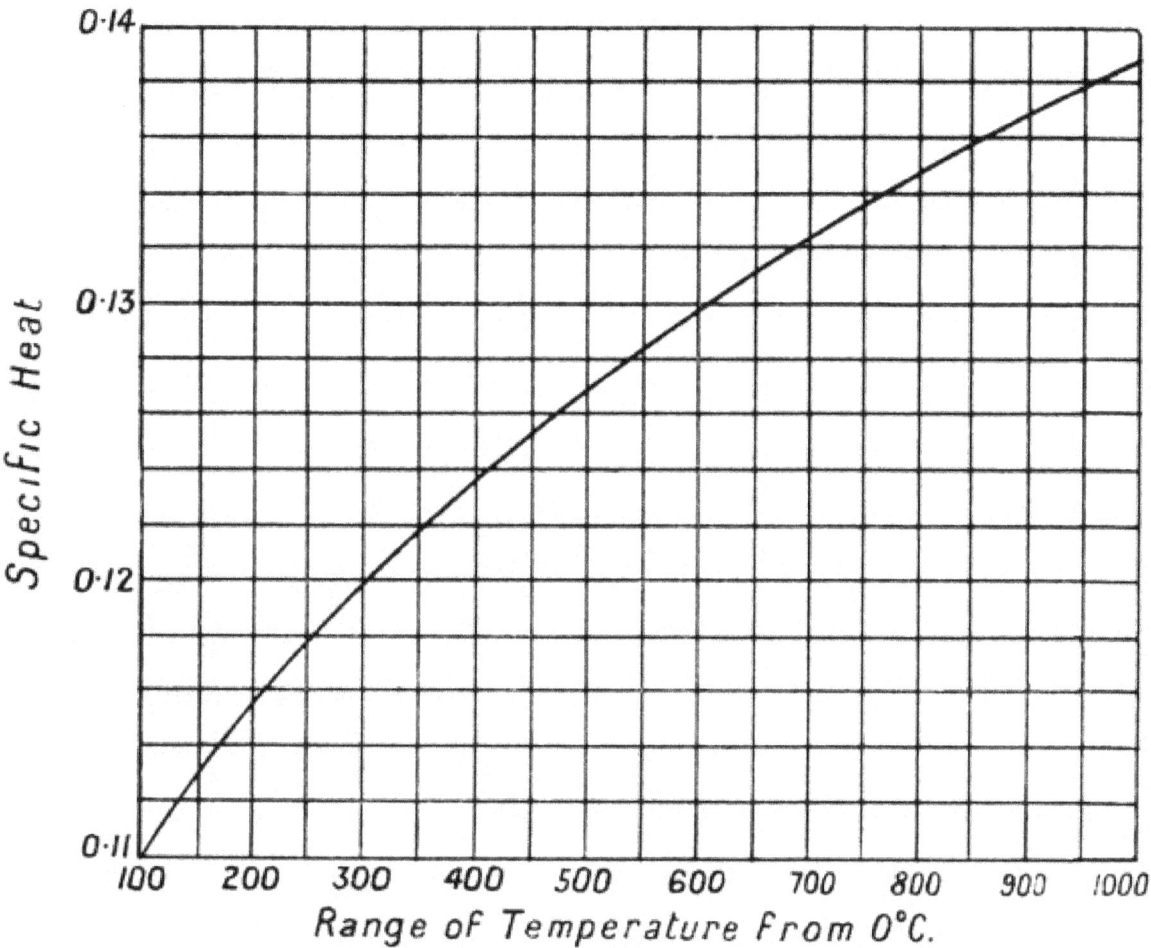

FIG. 65.—SPECIFIC HEAT OF NICKEL OVER RANGES FROM 0° C.

Regnault, who first suggested the calorimetric method for high temperature measurement, attempted to measure the specific heat of iron over different ranges, with a view to using this metal in the process. Owing to the absence of reliable means of determining the experimental temperatures, however, Regnault's values were considerably in error. For the range 0 to 1000° C. he gave the average specific heat of iron as 0·126, a figure much below the truth. Thus, if a piece of iron be heated to 970° C., as measured by the thermo-electric method, and dropped into water, the temperature calculated from an assumed specific heat of 0·126 will be found to be 1210°, or 240° too high. The values now employed are obtained by experiments with a thermo-electric pyrometer, so that temperatures deduced by the calorimetric method agree, within the limits of manipulative error, with those of the standard scale. The accompanying curve, fig. 65, shows the average specific heat of nickel over all ranges between 0° and 1000° C., and from this curve the correct figure to use in the calculation for any range may be determined. Thus for a furnace between 800° and 900° C. the specific heat would be taken as 0·136; and although the choice of the value to be taken involves a knowledge of the temperature within 100°, no difficulty arises in practice, as it is easy to judge this limit by experience at temperatures below 1000° C In the most approved forms of calorimetric pyrometers for industrial purposes the temperature of the hot metal may be read directly from a scale, prepared in accordance with the value applying to the specific heat at various ranges.

Copper and iron are still used to a limited extent in these pyrometers, but lose continuously in weight by oxidation, the scales of oxide falling off when quenched, necessitating weighing before each test to ensure accuracy. Nickel oxidises very little below 1000 C., and as the thin film of oxide which forms does not readily peel off, the weight may increase slightly. Quartz would probably be more suitable than metals, not being altered by heating and quenching, but does not appear to have been tried for this purpose. Another possible material is nichrom, which resists oxidation below 1000° C. The weight of the solid should be at least 1/20 of that of the water, in order to ensure a tangible rise in temperature, and the thermometer should be capable of detecting 1/20 of a degree C. The rise in temperature should not be so great as to cause the water to exceed the atmosphere in temperature by more than 4° or 5° C., as otherwise radiation losses would have a marked effect. The limits of accuracy of the method will be shown by reference to examples.

Example I.—A piece of nickel, weighing 100 grams, is placed in a furnace, and after heating dropped into 2000 grams of water at 10° C., contained in a vessel of water equivalent 50 grams. The temperature rises to 16·25° C. The specific heat of nickel for the range is 0·137. To find the temperature of the furnace and the limits of accuracy, the thermometer being readable to 1/20° C. Equating heat lost by the nickel to that gained by the water and vessel:—

$$100 \times 0·137 \times (x - 16·25) = 2050 \times (16·25 - 10·0)$$

from which $x = 952°$ C.

If the error in each thermometer reading amounted to $\frac{1}{40}°$ the maximum difference in the above calculation is obtained by introducing the altered values as under:—

$$100 \times 0·137 \times (x - 16·225) = 2050 \times (16·225 - 10·025)$$

when $x = 944°$ C.

The maximum error due to a possible incorrect reading of $\frac{1}{40}°$ is therefore less than 1 per cent.

Example II.—The loss of heat by radiation in transferring 100 grams of nickel at 927° C., possessing a surface of 30 square centimetres, and with radiating power 0·7 of a black body, may be shown by the fourth-power law to be 50 calories per second (see page 139). If two seconds were occupied in the transfer, the error from this cause would be 1 in 130; and adding this to the thermometric error, the total is less than 2 per cent.

Practical Forms of Calorimetric Pyrometers.—When required to estimate the temperature of a muffle furnace or other laboratory appliance, a sheet-copper vessel of about 1500 c.c. capacity may be used. This should rest on wooden supports in a second similar vessel, about 2 inches wider, which acts as a shield against radiation. A cylinder of nickel about 1½ inches long, and 1¼ inches in diameter, with a hole of ½-inch diameter in the centre, is suitable for test purposes. This may conveniently be heated in a nickel crucible; and when transferring to the water the crucible may be grasped with a pair of tongs, and tilted so as to allow the cylinder to drop into the water. When used in a tube furnace, a length of thin nickel wire may be attached to the cylinder to enable withdrawal to be accomplished rapidly, allowance being made for the weight of the heated wire. The transfer should be accomplished as speedily as possible, to avoid radiation errors. The figure to be used to represent the specific heat of nickel may be obtained from the curve (fig. 65), when the range to be measured is approximately known. The water equivalent of the vessel and thermometer should be determined as follows:—Place in the vessel one-half the quantity of cold water used in the experiment—say 750 c.c.—and note the temperature (t_1) after stirring with the thermometer. Then add an equal quantity of water at a temperature (t_2) about 10° higher than t_1 Mix thoroughly with the thermometer, and note the temperature of the mixture (t_3). Check results may be obtained by varying the proportions of cold and warm water, the total quantity always being equal to that used for quenching the hot nickel. If W_1 = the weight of cold water, and W_2 that of the warm, the water equivalent (x) is obtained from the equation

$$x = \frac{W_2(t_2 - t_3) - W_1(t_3 - t_1)}{t_3 - t_1}.$$

This figure represents the weight of water equal in thermal capacity to the vessel, and in a pyrometric measurement is added to the weight of water taken.

In industrial practice, it is desirable to dispense, if possible, with the necessity for calculations, so that a reading may be taken by an unskilled observer. The earliest form of calorimetric pyrometer, patented by Byström in 1862, consisted of a lagged zinc vessel into which a piece of platinum was dropped, and a table was provided from which the temperature of the furnace could be read by noting the rise in temperature of the water. The modern industrial form, made by Messrs Siemens, will now be described.

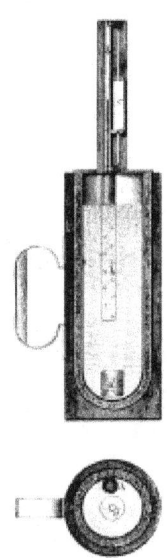

Fig. 66.—Siemens'
Calorimetric or
"Water" Pyrometer.

Siemens' Calorimetric or "Water" Pyrometer.—Fig. 66 shows this instrument in longitudinal and transverse section. It consists of a double copper vessel, the inner containing water, and the outer provided with a handle. The space between is lagged with felt, to prevent escape of heat from the water. The thermometer, b, is protected by a perforated brass tube from damage that might be caused on dropping in the hollow nickel cylinder, d. Opposite the stem of the thermometer is placed a sliding-piece c, on which a temperature scale is marked. In using the instrument, the specified quantity of water is placed in the inner vessel, and the pointer on c brought opposite to the top of the mercury column in the thermometer. The nickel cylinder, which has been heated in a crucible or muffle in the furnace, is then dropped in, and the vessel shaken to secure an equal temperature throughout the water. When the thermometer is stationary, the mark on c opposite the top of the mercury gives the temperature of the furnace, the scale on c having previously been marked from calculations made for each 50 degrees. The correctness of the reading evidently depends upon the accuracy with which c has been calibrated, an operation which involves taking into account the water equivalent of the vessel and the variation of the specific heat of nickel at different temperatures. Allowing for the sources of error attaching to the method, results by this pyrometer cannot be guaranteed to better than 2 or 3 per cent, at 900° or 1000° C., but in cases where this degree of inaccuracy is not of importance, the instrument may be used with advantage. As no calculation is necessary, the determination may be made in the workshop by any workman who exercises care in conducting the operation. Copper and iron cylinders are sometimes supplied instead of nickel, but are not to be recommended, as they decrease in weight with each test, and necessitate the use of a multiplying factor to convert the reading on c into the true temperature.

Special Uses of Calorimetric Pyrometers.—The great drawback to the calorimetric method is that each observation necessitates a separate experiment, involving time and labour. The accuracy, moreover, is not comparable with that obtainable by the use of a thermo-electric or resistance pyrometer; and practically the only recommendation is the low initial cost of the outfit. When an occasional reading of temperature, true to 3 per cent., suffices, the calorimetric pyrometer may be used; and in special laboratory determinations the method will frequently be found of value. Considering the low cost of thermo-electric pyrometers at the present time, it is probable that the calorimetric method will be entirely superseded in industrial practice, as the former method gives a continuous, automatic reading, and is capable of furnishing records. Many firms have already replaced their "water" pyrometers by the more accurate and useful appliances now available.

CHAPTER VIII
FUSION PYROMETERS

General Principles.—If a number of solids, possessing progressive melting points, be placed in a furnace and afterwards withdrawn, some may be observed to have undergone fusion whilst others would be unaffected. The temperature of the furnace would then be known to be higher than that of the melting point of the last solid melted, and lower than that of the first which remained intact. Taking, for example, a series of salts, the following might be used:-

Salt.	Melting Point.	
	Deg. Cent.	Deg. Fahr.
1 molecule common salt + 1 molecule potassium chloride	650	1202
Common salt	800	1472
Anhydrous sodium carbonate	850	1562
” ” sulphate	900	1652
Sodium plumbate	1000	1832
Anhydrous potassium sulphate	1070	1958
” magnesium sulphate	1150	2102

If, on inspection, it were found that the sodium sulphate had melted, whilst the sodium plumbate had survived, the temperature of the furnace would be known to lie between 900° C. and 1000° C. If a number of salts or other solids could be found with melting points ranging between 900° and 1000°, it would be possible to obtain a reading within narrower limits. The accuracy of the method in all cases is decided by the interval between the melting points of successive test materials.

Wedgwood, the famous potter, appears to have been the first to apply this method of determining the condition of a furnace, his test-pieces consisting of special clay compositions. The effect of the furnace on these was noted, and the suitability of the temperature for the work in hand deduced from the observations. Wedgwood in this manner investigated the variations in temperature at different levels in his firing-kilns, and was thus enabled to place the various wares at the positions best suited for their successful firing. Modern potters still use such test-pieces, as the information gained is not merely the degree of heat, but the effect of such heat on the articles undergoing firing. The fusion method, however, is now used to determine the temperature of all kinds of furnaces, and the chief modifications will now be described.

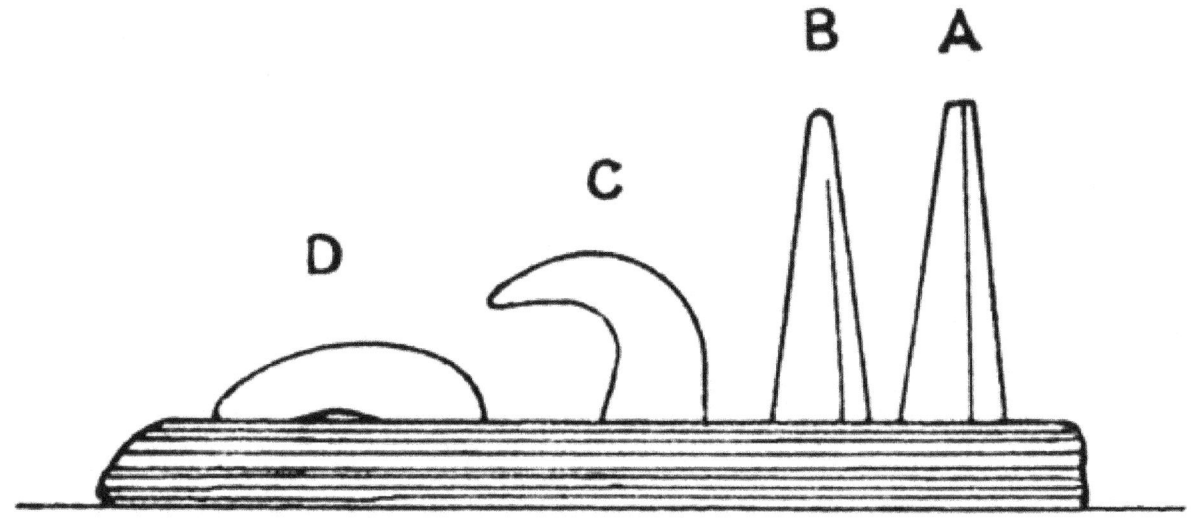

FIG. 67.—SEGER PYRAMIDS OR "CONES."

Seger Pyramids or "Cones."—Seger, of Berlin, published in 1886 an investigation dealing with the production of silicates of progressive melting points. By varying the composition, he was able to produce a series of materials with melting points ranging from 1890° C. to 590° C., the interval between successive compositions being 20° between 1890° and 950°, and 30° from the latter temperature to 590°. The highest member of the series has the composition Al_2O_3, SiO_2; and the lowest member $2SiO_2, B_2O_3$. For convenience in use the materials are made in the form of triangular pyramids, 5 cms. in height, and each side of the base 1·5 cms. long. Each pyramid is stamped with a distinguishing number, and altogether 60 are made to cover the range 1890° to 590°. When conducting a test, several pyramids are selected with melting points known to be near the temperature of the furnace, as discovered by previous trials. These are inserted in the furnace standing on a slab of refractory material, as in fig. 67, and may be watched through a sight-hole or withdrawn from the furnace for examination after attaining the existing temperature. If the right pyramids have been chosen, the appearance presented will be as in fig. 67, in which D is seen to have collapsed completely, C has bent over, B has been rounded at the top, whilst A is intact. The temperature of the furnace is then taken to correspond to the melting point of C, which is found by reference to a table in which the melting points corresponding to the different distinguishing numbers are given. The pyramids are extremely cheap, and only those with melting points near to the working temperature need be purchased. In cases where it is desired to increase the heat to a specified point, and then to allow the furnace to cool, these pyramids fulfil all requirements; an examination through a sight-hole closed with darkened glass enabling the furnace attendant to discover when the requisite temperature has been attained. The procedure is more difficult when it is desired to maintain a steady temperature, as this involves frequent renewal of pyramids already melted. These appliances are sold under the name of Seger "cones," the latter word being evidently a misnomer.

Watkin's Heat Recorder.—This arrangement consists of a small block of fireclay, having a number of cylindrical holes in its upper face. Pellets of materials of progressive melting points are placed in the holes, in which they fit loosely. The block is placed in the furnace, and afterwards withdrawn and examined, when those which have completely melted will be seen to have sunk, and to possess a concave surface; others which have been superficially fused, will show rounded edges, whilst others will be intact. The melting point of the highest member of the series which is observed to have rounded edges is taken as the temperature of the furnace. The materials used in the manufacture of the pellets are approximately the same as those employed by Seger, being the same in number (60), and differing progressively by similar intervals. It is not evident that the method of observation is superior to the use of pyramids, although some workers may prefer it, and the arrangement is merely an alternative plan of using the Seger compositions. Watkin has also introduced a modification in which straight bars of clay compositions are supported at the edges, the temperature being deduced by observing which numbers melt, droop, or remain intact.

"Sentinel" Pyrometers.—Under this name, Brearley, of Sheffield, has introduced a number of compositions, chiefly of salts, which possess definite melting points. These are made in the shape of cylinders, about 1 inch long and ¾ inch in diameter, which collapse completely when the melting point is attained. Compositions have been found which melt at certain temperatures known to give the best results in the treatment of different kinds of steel, and a cylinder of correct melting point, placed in the furnace on a small dish near to the steel, furnishes a simple and correct clue to the attainment of the desired temperature. The existing condition of a furnace may be discovered by taking a number of cylinders, having progressive melting points, and making observations after the manner described under the heading of Seger pyramids. A few "Sentinel" cylinders are frequently of use in the workshop or laboratory for other purposes, such as a rapid check of a given temperature in confirmation of the reading of an indicating pyrometer, or in discovering whether a certain temperature has been exceeded in a given case. "Sentinel" cylinders have been used in such a manner as to give audible warning of the attainment of a given temperature by means of a metal rod, which is made to rest on the cylinder, and which, when the cylinder melts, falls and completes the circuit of an electric bell. The upper range attainable by the use of ordinary metallic salts is not so great as in the case of silicates, but up to 1100° C. metallic sulphates, chlorides, etc., or mixtures of these, give results quite as good as those obtained with Seger pyramids.

Stone's Pyrometer.—This instrument is intended to indicate the correct temperature at which a metal or alloy should be poured, and consists of a silica tube at the bottom of which is placed an alloy melting at the temperature at which the material operated on should be poured. A silica rod rests on this alloy, and is connected at its upper end to an iron extension, the extremity of which engages a pointer moving over a scale. When the alloy in the silica tube melts, the rod falls through the molten mass and moves the pointer over the scale, thus giving a certain indication that the desired temperature has been attained. Arrangements exist for adjusting the pointer to zero at the commencement of a test.

Fusible Metals.—Instead of clays or salts, a number of metals and alloys are sometimes used. These are placed in the form of short rods in numbered holes in a piece of firebrick and inserted in the furnace, and on withdrawal those which have undergone fusion will be seen to have taken the form of the holes in which they were placed. The temperature of the furnace is considered to lie between the melting points of the last of the series to undergo fusion and the first which remains unchanged. A series of metals of this description is more costly than clays or salts, but is more rapid in action, owing to the superior conductivity of metals.

Fusible Pastes.—These consist of salts incorporated with vaseline or other suitable fat, and are used to detect the attainment of a specified temperature by a piece of metal. If, for example, it were desired to heat a piece of steel to 800° C. for a given purpose, a paste containing common salt might be smeared on its surface before placing in the furnace. On heating, the vaseline burns away, leaving a white mark due to the salt, and this white mark will be visible till the salt fuses. The disappearance of the white mark therefore indicates that the required temperature has been reached; and the method is simple and useful in cases where a number of articles are to be worked at a uniform temperature.

CHAPTER IX
MISCELLANEOUS APPLIANCES

Expansion and Contraction Pyrometers.—Most substances, on heating, exhibit an increase in size, and on cooling return to the original dimensions. If, however, a chemical alteration occur during the heating, the resultant material may be permanently altered in size, so that on cooling the substance may be of less or greater dimensions than before. Both these phenomena have been applied to the measurement of high temperatures; the permanent shrinkage undergone by clay being utilised by Wedgwood in the instrument which was the first practical pyrometer; the expansion of a solid by Daniell, and of liquid by Northrup. Both forms are still in use to a limited extent, and will now be described.

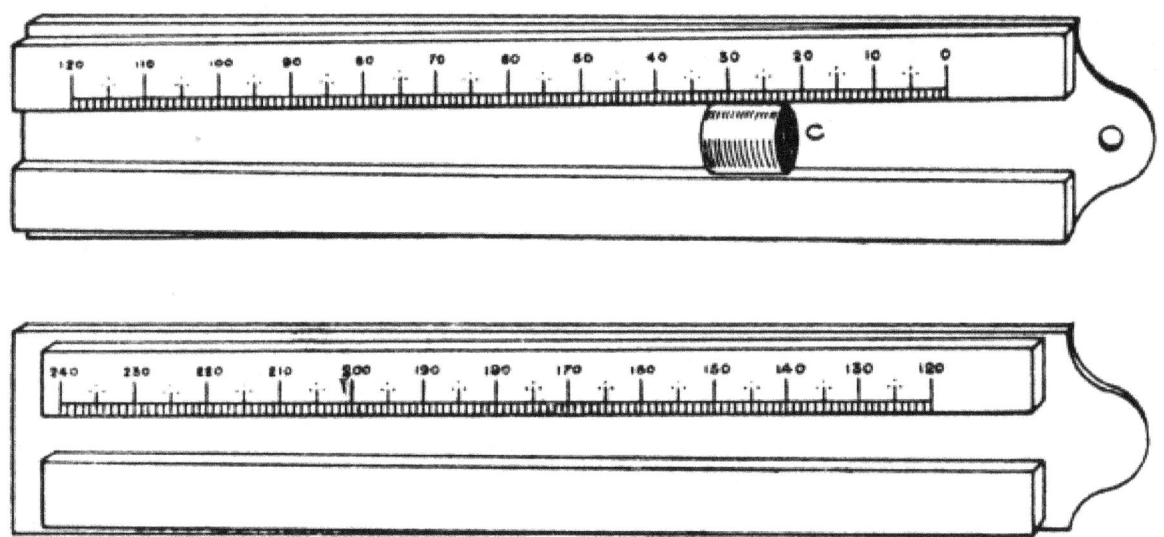

FIG. 68.—WEDGWOOD'S PYROMETER.

Wedgwood's Pyrometer.—In 1782 Wedgwood introduced a method of determining the condition of a furnace by observing the contraction shown by cylinders prepared from a special clay. The measuring device took the form of a tapered groove (fig. 68) made in two parts, each 6 inches long, and one a continuation of the other. Each inch of the groove was divided into 20 equal parts, making 240 divisions in all, and each division was called 1 degree. The width of the groove opposite the zero mark was 0·5 inch, and opposite 240, 0·3 inch. Before firing, the cylinders entered the groove until the lower end was opposite or near the zero mark; and after being inserted in the furnace and allowed to cool on removal, the cylinders were pushed as far as possible down the groove, when the mark opposite the lower end indicated the condition of the furnace in terms of Wedgwood's scale. The degrees were, of course, arbitrary; but with cylinders of uniform make a given position in the groove after heating always represented the same furnace temperature, and thus furnished an indication more reliable than the judgment of a workman's eye. Wedgwood attempted to express the divisions on his scale in terms of Fahrenheit degrees, and by extrapolation of results obtained at the highest limits of the mercury thermometer, where 1 degree of contraction was caused by a rise of 130° F., arrived at figures which now appear ludicrous, but which were accepted for forty years. As examples, the melting point of silver was given as 4717° F.; of cast iron, 17977° F.; and of wrought iron, 21637° F.—the last figure being nearly 19000° higher than the present accepted value of 2770° F. The error arose from the assumption of uniform contraction with increase of temperature, and furnishes a striking example of the danger of indefinite extrapolation from meagre data. But although the expression of the result in Fahrenheit degrees was so erroneous, the observed contraction always corresponded to a given condition of the furnace, and the firing was continued until that known to be the best for the work in hand was attained.

The permanent shrinkage referred to is caused by dehydration of the clay, and it therefore follows that this method can only give uniform results when exactly the same kind of clay is used for the test-pieces. A given manufacturer might secure consistent indications by making a quantity of clay, to be kept specially for this purpose; but the same contraction at a given temperature would not be obtained by a second observer who also had prepared a quantity of clay, as slight differences in composition cause large variations in the observed contraction. In practice, therefore, pyrometers of this type are not interchangeable, and each user must standardize for his own special conditions. Wedgwood's pyrometer is still used to a small extent; its replacement, however, by the more convenient and accurate instruments now available is only a question of time.

Daniell's Pyrometer.—In 1822 Daniell published an account of a pyrometer based on the expansion of a platinum rod enclosed in a plumbago tube. One end of the rod pressed against the end of the tube, whilst the other end was free to move, and was connected to a multiplying device which magnified the expansion, the increased movement being indicated by a pointer, moving over a dial. The scale on the dial was divided evenly into a suitable number of parts, it being assumed that the difference between the expansions of graphite and platinum was uniform at all temperatures. The scale was calibrated as far as possible by comparison with a mercury thermometer, the remainder being extrapolated. With this pyrometer Daniell obtained a value of 2233° F. for the melting point of silver, and 3479° F. for that of cast iron—results considerably higher than those now accepted, but much nearer than those obtained by Wedgwood. Daniell's pyrometer was widely used, and its modern representatives are fairly common. Platinum, owing to its cost, is no longer used in these instruments, which are now generally made with a graphite rod encased in an iron tube, on the end of which the graduated dial is placed, as shown in fig. 69. Another form, commonly used in baker's ovens, is constructed with an iron rod surrounded by a porcelain or fireclay tube.

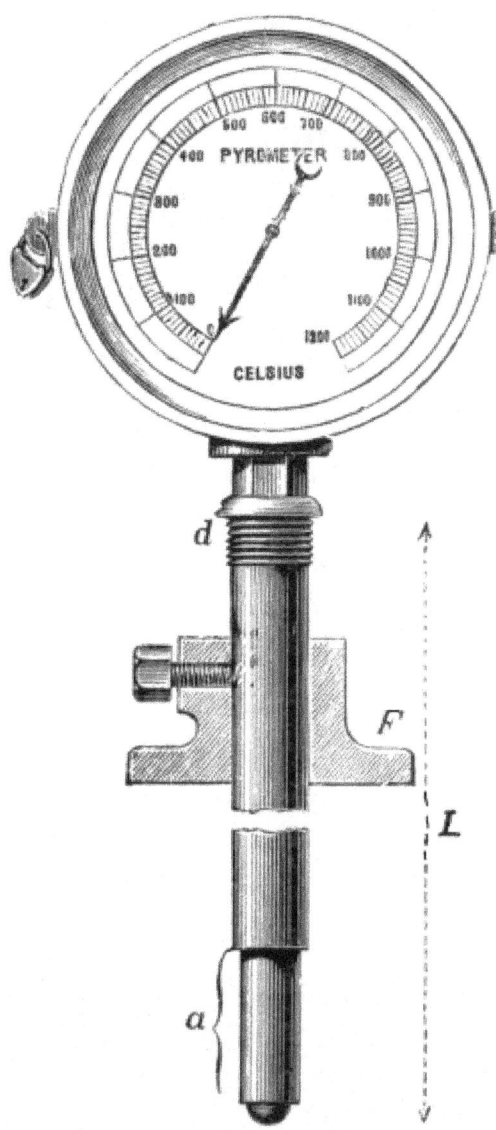

FIG. 69.—EXPANSION PYROMETER.

The defect of pyrometers of this type is that the coefficient of expansion of the materials alters with prolonged heating, causing the readings to become erroneous. Re-adjustment in boiling water or other substance does not compensate properly for this alteration, as both materials are not equally affected. Again, the readings will be too low unless the whole of the expanding parts are in the interior of the furnace, in which respect this pyrometer is inferior to a thermo-electric instrument, which may be inserted at any convenient depth, and may therefore be used for a greater variety of purposes. The chief recommendation is cheapness; but an expansion pyrometer should never be used for work of precision. A graphite rod in an iron enclosure gives more consistent results than other materials.

Northrup's Molten Tin Pyrometer.—Tin melts at 232° C., and boils at 2270° C. It does not give off vapour sensibly up to 1700° C., and expands with great uniformity. It is therefore suitable for measuring high temperatures on the same principle as an ordinary thermometer, and Dufour, in 1900, attempted to make a high-reading thermometer by enclosing tin in a silica bulb. Northrup has constructed an instrument in which the bulb and stem are of graphite, and the height of the molten tin is determined by lowering a nickel wire through a gland until it touches the tin, thereby completing an electric circuit and causing a bell to ring or producing a deflection on a galvanometer. The upper end of the nickel wire moves over a scale, which may be marked at two suitable fixed points, and the scale divided up as in the case of an ordinary thermometer. The durability of the graphite cover will determine the utility of this pyrometer, and protection by some good refractory will be essential to prevent oxidation. Such a pyrometer will not respond quickly to changes in temperature, but may prove useful in reading temperatures at ranges beyond the scope of present thermo-electric pyrometers. Northrup anticipates that this instrument may be used up to 1800° C.

Vapour-Pressure Pyrometers.—In these instruments mercury is placed in a stout steel tube, to which a pressure-gauge is attached, which registers the vapour-pressure of the mercury. Readings of pressure may be translated into temperatures by calibration with a standard pyrometer. The range of these instruments is limited—600° or 700° C.—and they are seldom used at present, having been superseded by more modern types.

Water-Jet Pyrometers.—In these instruments water is passed through a pipe placed in the furnace or hot space at a definite rate, and from the rise in temperature produced in the water that of the furnace may be obtained. An outfit of this kind entails the provision of a steady source of water-pressure, and the indications can only remain accurate so long as the bore of the pipe remains uniform. The calibration is made by comparison with a standard pyrometer. The drawbacks to the method are its inconvenience, and the necessity for continuous skilled supervision; and in consequence of these the arrangement is seldom used.

Pneumatic Pyrometers.—Attempts have been made to deduce furnace temperatures by blowing air at uniform pressure through a pipe located in the hot space, and noticing the increase in the temperature of the air. In the Uehling pyrometer, air from the hot space is drawn through an opening of fixed size by means of a steam-jet, which acts as an aspirator. The opening is placed at one end of a chamber, and the steam-jet aspirator at the other end; and a diaphragm with a central hole divides the chamber into two parts. The pressures existing in the two portions of the chamber vary according to the temperature of the air drawn in, and are measured by water-gauges, the readings of which may be translated into temperatures by calibration against a thermo-electric or other pyrometer. The method is ingenious, but is elaborate and costly; and is therefore little used.

Conduction Pyrometers.—If one end of a rod of metal be inserted in a furnace, heat will be conducted along it to the portion external to the furnace, and a steady condition will be obtained when the heat escaping from the external part of the rod, by convection and radiation, is equal to the quantity conducted along the rod. The hotter the portion in the furnace, the higher will be the temperature of all parts of the external length. A series of thermometers placed at intervals in the exterior portion would show a progressive fall in temperature along the rod; and the hotter the furnace the higher would be the reading on each thermometer. In applying this principle to the measurement of high temperatures, a bar of copper or iron is passed through the wall of the furnace, so that a length of 2 feet or more protrudes on the outside. Near the end of the external portion a hole is drilled to a sufficient depth to cover the bulb of a thermometer, which is inserted in the hole, into which a quantity of mercury is poured to make a metallic contact between the bulb and the bar. The reading of the thermometer furnishes an approximate clue to the temperature of the furnace, rising or falling with corresponding changes in the hot space. A calibration might be effected by comparison with a standard; but the method is only applied to the production of a prescribed condition, known by experience to be attained when the thermometer reading has a certain value—say 120° C. Changes in atmospheric temperature, or currents of air, seriously affect the readings, and the method at best is only approximate.

Gas Pyrometers.—Wiborgh, Bristol, and others have constructed pyrometers in which the pressure of an enclosed gas is recorded by a

Bourdon pressure-gauge, the scale of which is calibrated so as to read temperatures. A porcelain bulb, terminating in a capillary tube which is connected to the gauge, is used to contain the air or other gas; but at temperatures above a red heat the readings become uncertain, owing either to leakages or the distortion of the bulb. The most suitable material for the bulb (alloy of platinum, 80 per cent., and rhodium, 20 per cent.) is too costly to use industrially, and would deteriorate under the influence of furnace gases. In the Bristol recording instrument the moving index of the pressure-gauge terminates in a pen, which touches a chart-paper revolving by clockwork. Good results are obtained up to 400° C., but beyond this the indications are uncertain, and the instrument is more correctly described as a recording thermometer.

Wiborgh's Thermophones.—These consist of infusible clay cylinders, 2·5 cms. long and 2 cms. in diameter, which contain an explosive. When placed in a hot space, the explosion occurs after a definite time, the interval being less at high temperatures than at lower, as the rate at which heat is conducted through a solid varies directly as the difference between the external and internal temperatures. The interval elapsing between placing in the furnace and the subsequent explosion is noted on a stop-watch to the nearest 1/5 second, and from the observed time the temperature is obtained from a table, drawn up from the results of experiments under known conditions. If the cylinders be kept dry, an observer experienced in the use of thermophones may secure a reading to within 40° C.

Joly's Meldometer.—This device, due to Dr Joly, is intended for laboratory determinations of melting points. It consists of a strip of platinum, heated by electricity, upon which a tiny fragment of the material is placed, which is viewed through a microscope. The temperature of the platinum is regulated by means of a rheostat in the circuit, and in making a test the temperature is gradually raised until the material is observed to become globular, or to flow over the platinum strip. The temperature at which this occurs is deduced from the linear expansion of the platinum strip, which is measured by a micrometer attached to the instrument. When carefully used, very accurate determinations may be made by the meldometer, the results, moreover, being obtained rapidly, and with the use of the minimum of material.

Brearley's Curve Tracer.—This apparatus made by the Cambridge and Paul Instrument Company, is designed to take a large-scale record of an operation which only occupies a short period of time. It consists of a drum, round which the record paper is wound, and capable of rotating on its axis once in ten or thirty minutes by the aid of clockwork. Attached to the arm of the pen is a pointer, which moves along the scale of a sensitive mirror galvanometer to which a thermocouple is connected. The operator, by turning a handle, moves the drum longitudinally so as to keep the pointer opposite the centre of the spot of light, and this movement is traced on the chart, combined with the rotary movement, by the pen. In this manner the large change in deflection, due to a few degrees increase or decrease in temperature, can be recorded in ink. This instrument is of special service in recording the critical points of steel, or any operation which involves delicate readings over a limited range of temperature.

www.ingramcontent.com/pod-product-compliance
Lightning Source LLC
Chambersburg PA
CBHW081157020426
42333CB00020B/2537